ADAPTIVE 2022

The Fourteenth International Conference on Adaptive and Self-Adaptive Systems and Applications

April 24 - 28, 2022

Barcelona, Spain

ADAPTIVE 2022 Editors

Marc Kurz, University of Applied Sciences Upper Austria, Austria

Erik Sonnleitner, University of Applied Sciences Upper Austria, Austria

Printed from e-media with permission by:

Curran Associates, Inc.
57 Morehouse Lane
Red Hook, NY 12571

Some format issues inherent in the e-media version may also appear in this print version.

Printed with permission by Curran Associates, Inc. (2023)

International Academy, Research, and Industry Association (IARIA)
412 Derby Way
Wilmington, DE 19810

Phone: (408) 893-6407
Fax: (408) 527-6351

petre@iaria.org

Additional copies of this publication are available from:

Curran Associates, Inc.
57 Morehouse Lane
Red Hook, NY 12571 USA
Phone: 845-758-0400
Fax: 845-758-2633
Email: curran@proceedings.com
Web: www.proceedings.com

Table of Contents

MeUI - Machine Learning Enhanced Adaptive User Interaction 1
Marc Kurz and Erik Sonnleitner

Tree-Based Regressors for Predicting Energy Expenditure from Heart Rate in Wearable Devices 5
Stephan Selinger and Luka Dimitrijevic´

Context-Aware Security Intelligence of Vulnerability Scanners in Cloud-native Environments 10
Simon Ammer, Jens Krosche, Markus Gierlinger, and Mario Kahlhofer

Complex Responsive Processes in a Multi-Agent System: A Knowledge Accelerator 14
Guido Willemsen, Luis Correia, and Marco Janssen

Negligible Details - Towards Abstracting Source Code to Distill the Essence of Concepts 22
Christian Schindler, Mirco Schindler, and Andreas Rausch

Usage of Machine Learning for Subtopology Detection in Wire and Arc Additive Manufacturing 32
Dimitri Bratzel, Stefan Wittek, Andreas Rausch, Kai Treutler, Tobias Gehrling, and Volker Wesling

Towards A Data Marketplace Ecosystem 38
Sebastian Lawrenz, Priyanka Sharma, and Andreas Rausch

Qualitative Monitors based on the Connected Dependability Cage Approach 46
Felix Helsch, Iqra Aslam, Abhishek Buragohain, and Andreas Rausch

ADAPTIVE 2022

Forward

The Fourteenth International Conference on Adaptive and Self-Adaptive Systems and Applications (ADAPTIVE 2022), held on April 24 - 28, 2022, continued a series of events targeting advanced system and application design paradigms driven by adaptiveness and self-adaptiveness. With the current tendencies in developing and deploying complex systems, and under the continuous changes of system and application requirements, adaptation is a key feature. Speed and scalability of changes require self-adaptation for special cases. How to build systems to be easily adaptive and self-adaptive, what constraints and what mechanisms must be used, and how to evaluate a stable state in such systems are challenging duties. Context-aware and user-aware are major situations where environment and user feedback is considered for further adaptation.

The conference had the following tracks:

- Self-adaptation
- Adaptive applications
- Adaptivity in robot systems
- Fundamentals and design of adaptive systems
- Computational Trust for Self-Adaptive Systems
- Assurances and metrics for adaptive and self-adaptive systems

Similar to the previous edition, this event attracted excellent contributions and active participation from all over the world. We were very pleased to receive top quality contributions.

We take here the opportunity to warmly thank all the members of the ADAPTIVE 2022 technical program committee, as well as the numerous reviewers. The creation of a high quality conference program would not have been possible without their involvement. We also kindly thank all the authors that dedicated much of their time and effort to contribute to ADAPTIVE 2022. We truly believe that, thanks to all these efforts, the final conference program consisted of top quality contributions.

Also, this event could not have been a reality without the support of many individuals, organizations and sponsors. We also gratefully thank the members of the ADAPTIVE 2022 organizing committee for their help in handling the logistics and for their work that made this professional meeting a success.

We hope ADAPTIVE 2022 was a successful international forum for the exchange of ideas and results between academia and industry and to promote further progress in the area of adaptive and self-adaptive systems and applications. We also hope that Barcelona provided a pleasant environment during the conference and everyone saved some time to enjoy the historic charm of the city

ADAPTIVE 2022 General Chair

Jaime Lloret Mauri, Universitat Politecnica de Valencia, Spain

ADAPTIVE 2022 Steering Committee

Constantin Paleologu, University Politehnica of Bucharest, Romania
Claudia Raibulet, University of Milano-Bicocca, Italy
Sebastian Herold, Karlstad University, Department for Mathematics & Computer Science, Sweden
Andreas Rausch, TU Clausthal, Clausthal-Zellerfeld, Germany
Marc Kurz, University of Applied Sciences Upper Austria, Faculty for Informatics, Communications and Media, Austria
Valerie Camps, Paul Sabatier University - IRIT, Toulouse, France
Yukio Hayashi, Japan Advanced Institute of Science and Technology, Japan

ADAPTIVE 2022 Publicity Chair

Lorena Parra, Universitat Politecnica de Valencia, Spain
Javier Rocher, Universitat Politècnica de València, Spain

ADAPTIVE 2022

Committee

ADAPTIVE 2022 General Chair

Jaime Lloret Mauri, Universitat Politecnica de Valencia, Spain

ADAPTIVE 2022 Steering Committee

Constantin Paleologu, University Politehnica of Bucharest, Romania
Claudia Raibulet, University of Milano-Bicocca, Italy
Sebastian Herold, Karlstad University, Department for Mathematics & Computer Science, Sweden
Andreas Rausch, TU Clausthal, Clausthal-Zellerfeld, Germany
Marc Kurz, University of Applied Sciences Upper Austria, Faculty for Informatics, Communications and Media, Austria
Valerie Camps, Paul Sabatier University - IRIT, Toulouse, France
Yukio Hayashi, Japan Advanced Institute of Science and Technology, Japan

ADAPTIVE 2022 Publicity Chair

Lorena Parra, Universitat Politecnica de Valencia, Spain
Javier Rocher, Universitat Politècnica de València, Spain

ADAPTIVE 2022 Technical Program Committee

Habtamu Abie, Norwegian Computing Center/Norsk Regnesentral-Blindern, Norway
Harvey Alférez, Universidad de Montemorelos, Mexico
Raid Al-Nima, Northern Technical University, Iraq
Nik Bessis, Edge Hill University, UK
Glen Bright, University of KwaZulu Natal, Durban, South Africa
Antonio Brogi, University of Pisa, Italy
Barbara Buck, Boeing Global Services, USA
Valerie Camps, Paul Sabatier University - IRIT, Toulouse, France
Constantin F. Caruntu, "Gheorghe Asachi" Technical University of Iasi, Romania
Enrique Chirivella Perez, University West of Scotland, UK
Angel P. del Pobil, Jaume I University, Spain
Laura-Maria Dogariu, University Politehnica of Bucharest, Romania
Ibrahim Abdallah Abbas Atwa Elgendy, School of Computer Science and Technology | Harbin Institute of Technology, China
Holger Eichelberger, University of Hildesheim, Germany
Amgad Mohammed Elsayed, University of Deusto, Spain
Fairouz Fakhfakh, University of Sfax, Tunisia
Francisco José García-Peñalvo, University of Salamanca, Spain

Zhiwei Gao, Northumbria University, UK
Yukio Hayashi, Japan Advanced Institute of Science and Technology, Japan
Hongsheng He, Wichita State University, USA
Sebastian Herold, Karlstad University, Department for Mathematics & Computer Science, Sweden
Koen Hindriks, Vrije University Amsterdam, Netherlands
Christopher-Eyk Hrabia, Technische Universität Berlin | DAI-Labor, Germany
Marc-Philippe Huget, Polytech Annecy-Chambery-LISTIC | University of Savoie, France
Imène Jraidi, McGill University - ATLAS Lab, Canada
Yasushi Kambayashi, Nippon Institute of Technology, Japan
Michael Katchabaw, Western University, London - Ontario, Canada
Stephan Kluth, FOM Hochschule für Oekonomie & Management gemeinnützige Gesellschaft mbH, Germany
Marc Kurz, University of Applied Sciences Upper Austria - Faculty for Informatics, Communications and Media, Austria
Mikel Larrea, University of the Basque Country UPV/EHU, Spain
Rajini M., PES University, India
Mieke Massink, CNR-ISTI, Italy
James E. McCarthy, Instructional Systems - Sonalysts Inc., USA
René Meier, Lucerne University of Applied Sciences and Arts, Switzerland
Philippe Merle, University of Lille, France
Andreas Metzger, University of Duisburg-Essen, Germany
Filippo Neri, University of Napoli "Federico II", Italy
Karol Niewiadomski, University of Wuppertal, Germany
Ashley Oiknine, DCS Corporation / Army Research Laboratory / University of California, Santa Barbara, USA
Krzysztof Okarma, West Pomeranian University of Technology in Szczecin, Poland
Joanna Isabelle Olszewska, University of West Scotland, UK
Constantin Paleologu, University Politehnica of Bucharest, Romania
Marcin Pietron, University of Science and Technology in Cracow, Poland
Agostino Poggi, Università degli Studi di Parma, Italy
Rasha Abu Qasem, Technische Universität Kaiserslautern, Germany
Claudia Raibulet, University of Milano-Bicocca, Italy
Andreas Rausch, TU Clausthal, Clausthal-Zellerfeld, Germany
Ruben Ricart Sanchez, University West of Scotland, UK
Oliver Roesler, Vrije Universiteit Brussel, Belgium
Joerg Roth, Nuremberg Institute of Technology, Germany
José Santos Reyes, University of A Coruña, Spain
Jagannathan (Jag) Sarangapani, Missouri University of Science and Technology, USA
Ichiro Satoh, National Institute of Informatics, Japan
Melanie Schranz, Lakeside Labs GmbH, Austria
Vasco N. G. J. Soares, Instituto de Telecomunicações / Instituto Politécnico de Castelo Branco, Portugal
Erik Sonnleitner, University of Applied Sciences Upper Austria - Faculty for Informatics, Communications and Media, Austria, Germany
Mohammad Divband Soorati, University of Southampton, UK
Cristian-Lucian Stanciu, University Politehnica of Bucharest, Romania
Roy Sterritt, Ulster University, UK
Justyna Swidrak, August Pi & Sunyer Biomedical Research Institute (IDIBAPS), Barcelona, Spain / Institute of Psychology - Polish Academy of Sciences, Warsaw, Poland

MeUI - Machine Learning Enhanced Adaptive User Interaction

Marc Kurz
University of Applied Sciences Upper Austria
Department of Mobility & Energy
4232 Hagenberg, Austria
email:marc.kurz@fh-hagenberg.at

Erik Sonnleitner
University of Applied Sciences Upper Austria
Department of Mobility & Energy
4232 Hagenberg, Austria
email:erik.sonnleitner@fh-hagenberg.at

***Abstract*—This position/vision paper describes the idea of a novel approach/research agenda of interacting with mobile devices. Usually, users have to learn how to interact with a mobile device adhering to rules that need to be learned. We intend to challenge and question this approach – we rather want the device to adapt to the needs and the behavior of the user. Thus, the idea is to use machine learning and artificial intelligence technologies to reverse the core principal of device utilization by providing a distinct, personalized and dynamically self-adaptive foundation towards modern human computer interaction. This position paper summarizes the core idea, provides an overview of related work and identifies and discusses research challenges.**

***Index Terms*—Mobile device interaction; human computer interaction; machine learning, adaptive user interfaces**

I. Introduction

Machine-Learning (ML) [1] and more generally Artificial Intelligence (AI) [2] are ever more present in different disciplines and industries. Disruptive innovations [3] change established technologies and markets, whereas - very often - ML and AI play a vital role in this phenomenon. Examples for such disruptive innovations are *Uber* [4], *Spotify* [5] or *Netflix* [6]. All of them build upon a strong fundament of massive data that is being processed with different AI/ML approaches in order to maximize the user experience and comfort. This allows for the advent of new technological innovations opening new markets and business models.

The core idea of this position paper entitled *MeUI – Machine-Learning Enhanced Adaptive User Interaction* intends to challenge the classic approach of interacting with mobile devices [7], [8]. Usually, users have to determine how to interact with a device adhering to rules that need to be learned. Following the trend of maximizing user experience and user comfort by radical new technological approaches, the idea is to use ML/AI technologies to reverse the core principal of device utilization by providing a distinct, personalized and dynamically self-adaptive foundation towards modern human computer interaction [9]–[11].

The rest of the paper further discusses this idea and provides an overview of conceivable use-cases that would allow for reversing this traditional approach of interacting with mobile devices. Furthermore, research challenges are defined consisting of hypotheses and questions that build the base for this novel approach. Since this is meant to be a position/vision paper, the authors strongly believe that this is a novel approach and has potential to radically transform the field of research of mobile device interaction by reversing the classic one-size-fits all approach to a personalized experience and that the discussed interaction aspect could build a fundamental new scientific field in the broader area of human machine/mobile interaction.

The rest of the paper is structured as follows. Section II discusses relevant use-cases, section III identifies the core research challenges and formulates research questions. In section IV potential methodological approaches are discussed and section V closes the paper with a conclusion and outlook.

II. Specific Conceivable Use-Cases

Although interface design and user experience are both important and long-standing branches [12]–[14] within product design on a broad scale, the elemental concept of such interfaces remains to reflect a learning task for the users with varying learning curves. Individual needs and requirements, such as disabilities or impairments [15], but also custom usage habits are hardly taken into account. Moreover, situational factors like body posture during certain activities, general body physique, location and more generally the context of the users [16] and the form factor of different devices may dramatically alter the requirements towards design, composition and organization of user interfaces.

With those non-ideal conditional factors in mind, modern machine-learning methodologies can help to acquire an understanding of how a user actually uses a device, including the detection and adaption to erratic behaviour and the repeated inversion of particular tasks or steps (e.g., repeatedly typing a particular character, while immediately afterwards deleting it again in order to type the correct one). Furthermore, the general adaptation of the keyboard on different mobile devices for specific users constitute the first relevant use-case: **UC1: Self-Learning Keyboard Adaptation**. The keyboard for textual input is adapted to the specific needs of the users - whereas this adaptation could range from simply highlighting specific characters (e.g., by resizing or colouring) to a different keyboard layout optimized for the user's habits.

Among other use-cases, certain interface elements, such as buttons and sliders may not be placed and scaled in the optimal and most efficient way possible for the behavioural characteristics of the utilizing person. For example, certain clickable elements may be out of reach for single-handed use, or sliders may be placed along the entire width of the available screen-space which may result in particular areas not being reachable in a comfortable way. On the other hand, slider elements which provide a horizontal scale being too narrow can undermine the precision required in order to set desired values. Interface configuration parameters like scrolling speed and, if supported by the respective device, touch sensitivity resemble adjustable values whose configuration may also be subject to being configured autonomously after a machine-learning algorithm has learned how the user likes to handle a device. This recomposition of interface components according to a specific user is the second relevant use-case: **UC2: Adaptive Interface Component Recomposition**.

Another specific use case worth mentioning tackles the ordering and grouping of applications on mobile devices. Recent studies show that users in Germany usually have around 90 apps installed on their smart phones but use only around 30 of them [17]. Furthermore, specific apps are only used on dedicated occasions (e.g., when travelling) - thus, besides other personal data, the context of the user could be an important factor regarding preferences for specific applications. If an intelligent component built from AI/ML technologies would manage to order and group applications autonomously according to the user's behaviour and context, user experience could increase dramatically. This aspect constitutes the third specific use-case: **UC3: Personalized and Context-Aware App Arrangement**.

Generally, the traditional one-size-fits-all approach of the past decades which aims to treat all users the same regardless of their needs has shown to coerce users to adapt their behaviour according to device expectations, while we believe that machine learning and AI approaches may in fact reverse this procedure and allow devices to adapt to their users.

Summarized, within the idea we intend to focus on the following specific use-cases that have been described above (whereas of course further relevant use-cases are imaginable and thus are not excluded from being investigated):

- **UC1:** Self-Learning Keyboard Adaptation
- **UC2:** Adaptive Interface Component Recomposition
- **UC3:** Personalized and Context-Aware App Arrangement

III. Research Challenges

Generally, the following hypothesis and research questions build the foundation for the approach of reversing the traditional way of interacting with mobile devices, whereas the three use-cases described above build the core baseline for these challenges:

- **Hypothesis**: ML/AI technologies allow for a significant change in the (mobile) device interaction in terms of usability. The classic approach of one-size-fits-all approach can be reversed towards a personalized experienced and a self-learning adaptation of interaction increasing the user experience.
- **RQ I**: which ML/AI technologies are suited for enhancing mobile device interaction?
- **RQ II**: to what extent can the user experience be improved focusing on the three described use-cases?
- **RQ III**: which differences concerning different mobile devices (e.g., smart phones and tablets) are relevant when improving the customer interaction with ML/AI technologies?
- **RQ IV**: which data and contextual information of the user is relevant for improving the customer interaction based on a self-learning ML/AI approach?

More and more people tend to use their mobile phone on a daily basis, which transforms the device into a constant companion [18]. With the advent of global interconnected mobile-devices, which offer significant computational power, applications running on mobile phones could gather huge information about the user. Thus, we believe that it is possible to turn the device into a self-adaptable, user-specific device that is constantly adapting to the user's needs and also the user's context [19] in order to maximize the customer experience and device-interaction. To the best of our knowledge this is a novel approach and has potential to radically transform the field of research of mobile device interaction by reversing the classic one-size-fits all approach to a personalized experience. We believe that the combination of ML/AI technologies with the discipline of human-computer interaction opens a new research field and has potential to (i) raise new research questions, (ii) to radically change the paradigm of interacting with mobile devices, and (iii) to build the foundation for a new era of technological inventions. The following paragraph summarizes the transformative potential of the idea.

A. *Transformative potential*

Long-established research concerning user interfaces and experiences primarily focused on the static and global layout structure as well as element selection, placement and feedback characteristics in order to create efficiently utilizable UIs, without taking the individual user needs into account. Longing for major progress within this field of research may consequently create an entire new niche of research questions and applications relevant to UX researchers as well as software development and manufacturing companies on a global scale. The currently predominant understanding of having to learn and adapt to predefined interfaces rather than smart devices getting used to how users actually employ, avail and devote to interfaces not only needs to be questioned but may also see a paradigm-shifting amendment in terms of how the interaction between humans and computers can be shifted towards a cooperative, device-reactive accommodation in the near future.

As an example, whereas some major manufacturers of smart mobile devices have gone through a development during the last decade, where they started to present their users a personalized user experience in terms of what information will be displayed when certain actions are performed. These advancements, however, merely represent a contentual and data-driven personalization rather than changing the elemental opportunities of device usage to the user's benefits and needs. A novel modal approach, restructuring and renewing the prototypical concept of the actual interfaces by allowing them to change and adapt dynamically allows us to move post the archetypical one-size-fits-all approaches regarding human-computer interaction in general, and user interfaces in particular by making software learn from and adapt to needs, adjust to and correct input errors and provide a meaningful and assisting individualization for every user. Using ML/AI technologies, the device has to gain knowledge of how it is used, rather than to dictate it.

IV. Research Methodology

In order to investigate the hypothesis as well as the intended research questions as stated in the previous section, the following methodological approach seem to be applicable. First and foremost, relevant mobile devices of different kinds and manufacturers (e.g., smart phones, tablets) have to be identified and their suitability for the different use-cases needs to be secured. For example, it needs to be clarified, if the keyboard layout can be easily changed - in case this is not necessary, a self-implemented keyboard mockup for evaluation can be developed. In detail, the most prevalent devices seem to be relevant, like (i) Apples iPhone, (ii) Android phones (e.g., Google Pixel 3, Samsung Galaxy S10), (iii) Apples iPad, (iv) Samsung Galaxy Tab.

Fundamental implementations on the intended different devices need to be done in order to enable the planned use-cases. Furthermore, ML/AI technologies need to be researched for investigating the suitability of the intended use-cases. In detail, *classical* approaches (e.g., Support Vector Machines (SVM), Naive Bayes, k-Nearest Neighbors (KNN) and Random Forest) [20] will be considered, as well as neural networks, deep learning [21] and long-short-term memory [22]. This is closely related to the identification of relevant user- and contextual-data that is of high value for the intended approach. Prototypical implementations of the use cases will be subject for user-studies and evaluations. The following Figure 1 illustrates the targeted steps for the research approach.

Summarized, the following methodological fragments need to be considered and constitute the base for the proposed research plan:

(i) Mobile device eligibility evaluation
(ii) User data identification and ML/AI technological qualification
(iii) Prototypical realization of the three identified use-cases
(iv) Conducting experiments and user-studies
(v) Evaluation of hypothesis and research questions
(vi) Identification of future potential and use cases

As it can be seen in 1 we intend to identify future potentials and also novel UX research paradigms by following the idea of reversing the traditional approach of mobile user interaction.

A. Risks and Challenges

The landscape of modern smartphone operating systems is rather limited, with only two major systems running on 98% of all such devices. As such, the applicability of dynamically adaptive interfaces may not be able to function on its full extent due to the fact of backend services and frameworks limiting the degree of freedom towards running applications (*apps*) when changing essential elements like GUI widgets at runtime. In such cases, the desired adaptability has to be either integrated through a transparent virtualized UI emulation layer, or by using technological capabilities beyond regular apps in order to acquire the desired results.

One such possibility would be to chose web-applications, whose UI elements consist largely of locally rendered HTML output which can elegantly be manipulated at runtime, even when the user is currently using the application – so-called *Progressive Web Apps*. While showing several major advantages compared to regular apps, progressive web-apps do not provide the capabilities of mobile operating systems in its entirety, by, e.g., not being allowed to access various hardware elements like I/O devices and sensors.

Another risk regarding technological feasibility is the possibility to manipulate tightly integrated and security-relevant core components like software keyboards. These are, at least in the case of Apple's iOS, not easily interchange- or manipulatable. Such limitations could be bypassed easily by creating dedicated applications for testing and evaluation purposes only, while not directly conveniently and efficiently suitable to be used by either third party applications, or any other native applications at all. Despite the fact that this may represent a potential outcome, the subsequent learning potential regarding the insights gained during research would unequivocally be of intrinsic significance, like described below.

B. Learning potential in case of failure

Failures within this research approach can be twofold, either technically or regarding the conceptual methodology of our main hypothesis.

If the technical evaluation proves that our approach provides benefit to users, but is not applicable to the current technical opportunities and status of mobile operating systems, having gained the expected knowledge advancements about ML-enhanced interfaces will hopefully start a discussion about how programmers and manufacturers can remove these limitations and barriers in order to allow more individualized device handling. If the prototypes manage to effectively show a major benefit towards user experience, a measurable decrease of erratic usage and an increased degree of contentment among device users, leading to a heightened awareness within both, the research community as well as commercial providers of frameworks and operating systems, the latter are expected to realize and appreciate the potential augmentation of market value and customer satisfaction and eventually begin to include the technical foundations needed to proceed.

If, however, our principal hypothesis along with the research questions proves to be incorrect, we gain insight into the

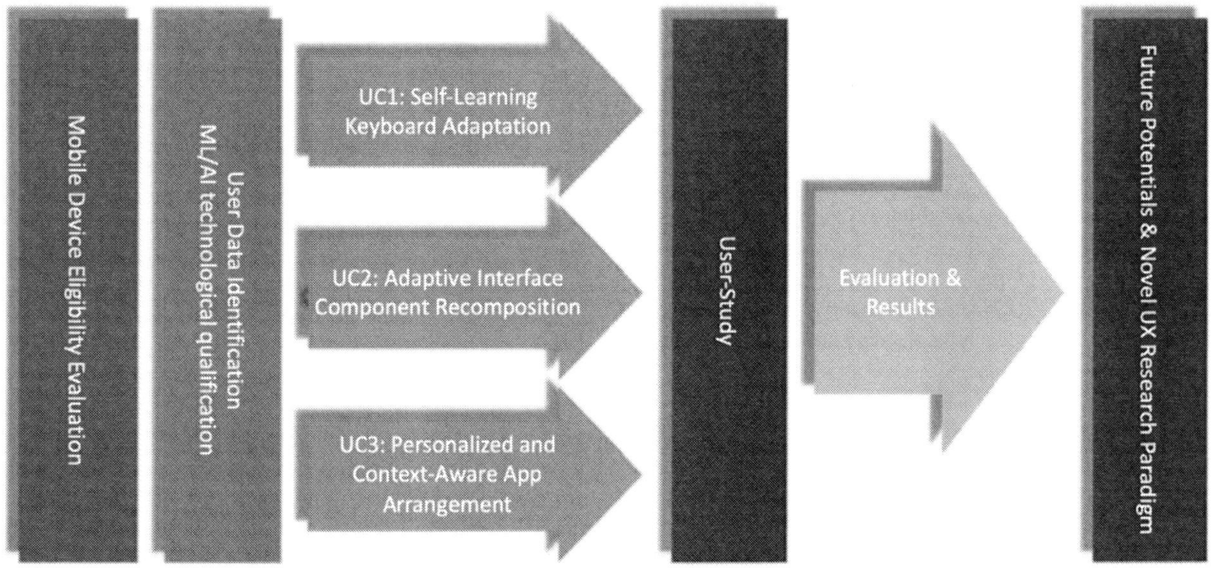

Fig. 1. The methodological aspects constituting the research agenda.

particular reasons thereof using the data and evaluation results generated during the pathway of our research and can hence help to steer further community efforts into different directions which may nevertheless incorporate various findings.

V. CONCLUSION

In our position/vision paper we presented the idea of reversing the classic approach of mobile user interaction. Instead having users to learn interaction and thus adapt to the mobile device, we envision systems that instead adapt to the user in an intelligent way, allowing to interact in the most possible intuitive way. Mobile device technology nowadays is able to deliver a variety of relevant user and context data - with machine learning and artificial intelligence mechanism it is our believe that smart devices can become really "smart" by adapting to the user. This aspect is perfectly summarized in our postulated hypothesis:

ML/AI technologies allow for a significant change in the (mobile) device interaction in terms of usability. The classic approach of one-size-fits-all approach can be reversed towards a personalized experienced and a self-learning adaptation of interaction increasing the user experience.

We have presented a research agenda constructed around identified use-cases. We intend to investigate our hypothesis in order to identify future potentials and also to put novel UX research paradigms on the table.

REFERENCES

[1] D. Michie, D. J. Spiegelhalter, and C. C. Taylor, "Machine learning, neural and statistical classification," vol. 13, 1994.
[2] S. J. Russell and P. Norvig, *Artificial intelligence: a modern approach*. Malaysia; Pearson Education Limited,, 2016.
[3] C. M. Christensen, *The innovator's dilemma: when new technologies cause great firms to fail*. Harvard Business Review Press, 2013.
[4] Uber Technologies Inc., https://www.uber.com, 2022 (accessed April 6, 2022).
[5] Spotify AB, https://www.spotify.com, 2022 (accessed April 6, 2022).
[6] Netflix, Inc., https://www.netflix.com, 2022 (accessed April 6, 2022).
[7] A. K. Karlson, B. B. Bederson, and J. Contreras-Vidal, "Understanding single-handed mobile device interaction," *Handbook of research on user interface design and evaluation for mobile technology*, vol. 1, pp. 86–101, 2006.
[8] J. Roth, "Patterns of mobile interaction," *Personal and Ubiquitous Computing*, vol. 6, no. 4, pp. 282–289, 2002.
[9] J. Preece, Y. Rogers, H. Sharp, D. Benyon, S. Holland, and T. Carey, *Human-computer interaction*. Addison-Wesley Longman Ltd., 1994.
[10] A. Dix, *Human-computer interaction*. Springer, 2009.
[11] S. K. Card, *The psychology of human-computer interaction*. Crc Press, 2018.
[12] J. Gong, P. Tarasewich *et al.*, "Guidelines for handheld mobile device interface design," in *Proceedings of DSI 2004 Annual Meeting*, 2004, pp. 3751–3756.
[13] N. Ocak and K. Cagiltay, "Comparison of cognitive modeling and user performance analysis for touch screen mobile interface design," *International Journal of Human–Computer Interaction*, vol. 33, no. 8, pp. 633–641, 2017.
[14] L. Punchoojit and N. Hongwarittorrn, "Usability studies on mobile user interface design patterns: a systematic literature review," *Advances in Human-Computer Interaction*, vol. 2017, 2017.
[15] Z. Sarsenbayeva, N. van Berkel, C. Luo, V. Kostakos, and J. Goncalves, "Challenges of situational impairments during interaction with mobile devices," in *Proceedings of the 29th Australian Conference on Computer-Human Interaction*. ACM, 2017, pp. 477–481.
[16] A. K. Dey, "Context-aware computing," in *Ubiquitous computing fundamentals*. Chapman and Hall/CRC, 2018, pp. 335–366.
[17] A. Annie, "The state of mobile in 2019," Jan. 2019.
[18] M. Kurz, B. Hiesl, and E. Sonnleitner, "Real-time activity recognition utilizing dynamically on-body placed smartphones," in *The Eleventh International Conference on Adaptive and Self-Adaptive Systems and Applications (ADAPTIVE 2019)*, 2019.
[19] T. Lemlouma and N. Layaida, "Context-aware adaptation for mobile devices," in *IEEE International Conference on Mobile Data Management, 2004. Proceedings. 2004*. IEEE, 2004, pp. 106–111.
[20] R. O. Duda, P. E. Hart, and D. G. Stork, *Pattern classification*. John Wiley & Sons, 2012.
[21] Y. LeCun, Y. Bengio, and G. Hinton, "Deep learning," *nature*, vol. 521, no. 7553, pp. 436–444, 2015.
[22] S. Hochreiter and J. Schmidhuber, "Long short-term memory," *Neural computation*, vol. 9, no. 8, pp. 1735–1780, 1997.

Tree-Based Regressors for Predicting Energy Expenditure from Heart Rate in Wearable Devices

Stephan Selinger
Department of Mobility and Energy
University of Applied Sciences Upper Austria
Hagenberg, Austria
email: stephan.selinger@fh-hagenberg.at

Luka Dimitrijević
Department of Mobility and Energy
University of Applied Sciences Upper Austria
Hagenberg, Austria
email: luka.dimitrijevic@students.fh-hagenberg.at

***Abstract*—Estimating energy expenditure from heart rate usually relies on population-based multiple linear regression equations, taking heart rate, age, gender, mass, height and, if available, VO_{2max} into account. In this paper, we show that non-linear models, such as random forests and regression trees are suited for the deployment on memory constrained wearable devices and assess physical activity more accurately than linear regression models. We fitted linear regression models, regression trees, and random forests with data from 892 graded exercise tests on a treadmill with 857 participants and evaluated their performance, as well as memory consumption on a PineTime smartwatch and an Apple Watch. A regression tree with a tree depth of 11 performed the same ($R^2 = 0.825$) as a widely used linear model by Keytel ($R^2 = 0.821$) but does not depend on VO_{2max}, which can be relevant for amateur athletes. The additional memory on the PineTime smartwach needed to store the tree increased the the original firmware size of 390 KiB to 416 KiB. If VO_{2max} is available, then a tree with a depth of 11 achieves a coefficient of 0.877, and the total memory size is 418 KiB.**

***Keywords*—energy expenditure; heart rate; regression tree; random forest regressor; wearable device**

I. INTRODUCTION

The importance of physical activity resulting in energy expenditure (EE) [1] for the prevention of non-communicable diseases, such as cardiovascular diseases and type 2 diabetes, as well as the link between exercise and longevity has long been well documented [2] [3] and validated over many decades [4]. The protective effects of exercise also enhances the immune response against bacteria and viruses [5].

Assessing EE as accurately as possible is not only relevant in the global context of health, but also for the automatic generation and adaptation of nutrition plans for athletes [6] and for individuals planning and tracking weight loss [7] [8].

Besides indirect calorimetry, heart rate measurement and accelerometry, or a combination of both, are popular methods for estimating EE [1] [9], and consequently, physical activity. Based on the assumption of a linear relationship between heart rate and oxygen consumption (VO_2), EE can be estimated from heart rate. Such a relationship is obtained by deriving a linear regression equation with EE being the dependent variable, and heart rate, age, gender, body mass, height, etc., the independent ones which can then be used to estimate VO_2 or EE in day-to-day living conditions [1].

Since this relationship is not always linear [10], it seems promising to investigate whether non-linear regression methods, such as random forests and regression trees which, from a computational point of view, are still feasible for the deployment on wearable devices, allow to more accurately predict EE rather than linear regression models.

The remainder of this paper is structured as follows: in Section II we review the related work, in Section III we describe the study design, then we continue with a discussion of results in Section IV, and conclude with Section V, in which we briefly summarize our findings and discuss possible future work.

II. RELATED WORK

Keytel et al. [11] provide two equations for predicting EE based on heart rate, age, gender, body mass, and optionally VO_{2max}. The first equation K_1 takes into account VO_{2max}, with which the results – not surprisingly – have a higher coefficient of determination ($R^2 = 0.821$). The second one, K_2, without a fitness measure might be more universal, however, at the cost of a lower coefficient ($R^2 = 0.737$).

Additionally, taking resting heart rate into account, Charlot et al. [12] achieve a coefficient of determination which is higher ($R^2 = 0.809$) than the Keytel equation without VO_{2max}, but slightly lower than the Keytel equation with VO_{2max}. However, incorporating resting heart rate and real-time running speed resulted in $R^2 = 0.919$. Even using running speed without heart rate outperforms the Keytel equations ($R^2 = 0.913$). However, this obviously limits the applicability to only running activities.

While the previous described approaches rely solely on heart rate and linear regression, Ellis et al. use values from hip and wrist mounted accelerometers and measured heart rate to train a regression forest [13]. In addition, they also perform activity classification. In their evaluation, Ellis et al. focus on performance only and leave the question about tree depth and the number of estimators in a random forest and consequently memory consumption unanswered.

III. TOOLS AND METHODS

As a starting point and to define a baseline, we fitted two linear regression equations using *scikit-learn* (version 0.22) [14], a Python library and compared it with the approaches described by Keytel et al. [11] and Charlot et al. [12]. Subsequently, we trained random forest and decision tree regressors and evaluated their performance, not only in regards to the obtained coefficients of determination and mean absolute error, but also in terms of memory demand. To that end, using an open-source code generation tool, *m2cgen* [15], we generated C-code from the previously trained regressors for the open-source smartwatch *PineTime* [16], which resembles a contemporary wearable device with an ARM Cortex-M4 CPU with 512 KiB of Flash and 64 KiB of RAM, capable of measuring heart rate based on photoplethysmography; other sensors include an accelerometer.

In addition, to investigate which coefficient of determination can be achieved on a fairly unconstrained device, we also deployed the previously trained models to an Apple Watch SE (2020) running watchOS 8.3. The watch is considered a powerful device in comparison to the PineTime because of its 1 GiB of RAM and as 32 GiB of storage capacity and a custom dual core CPU which also contains dedicated hardware which can help streamline machine learning tasks. Like the open-source watch, it is also capable of measuring heart rate with an optical sensor; an accelerometer is present here as well.

A. Participants and Graded Exercise Tests

In our study, we used a publicly available database provided by the Exercise Physiology and Human Performance Lab of the University of Malaga [17] [18] [19]. In addition to other measurements, the database contains heart rate, oxygen consumption, carbon dioxide generation, and treadmill speed from 857 amateur and professional athletes (149 females, 708 males) performing 992 graded exercise tests. After a warm-up period of 5 minutes with 5 km/h, treadmill speed was periodically increased by 0.5 or 1 km/h intervals until exhaustion after which the speed was reduced back to the initial 5 km/h. The demographic characteristics of the participants are given in Table I.

TABLE I
DEMOGRAPHIC CHARACTERISTICS.

Variable	*Range*	*Median*	*Interquartile Range*
Age (years)	10 - 63	27.1	15.2
Body mass (kg)	41 - 135	73.0	14.0
Height (cm)	150 - 203	175.0	10.0
VO_{2max} (ml/kg/min)	22.4 - 86.9	52.4	12.7

B. Fitting the Regressors

Before splitting the data into a training (75 %) and test data set (25 %) we calculated EE in KJ from O_2 and VO_2 according to the Weir formula [20]. Next, with different combinations of the independent variables listed below, we fitted two linear models to predict EE:

- LM_1: heart rate, age, weight, and gender; this is comparable to K_2.
- LM_2: same as LM_1, additionally VO_{2max}; comparable to K_1.

Regression trees were first fitted using the default hyper parameters provided by scikit-learn to determine the maximum tree depth which, as expected, exceeded the available memory on the PineTime. Therefore, we reduced the tree depth to a value that gave the same, or even a slightly better performance than linear model LM_1. From that point on, we increased the tree depth until the available memory was exhausted again. During that process we not only observed the influence of the tree depth based on our test data set, but also on the training data set to assess possible over-training (see Figure 1):

- RT_1: Regression tree with sckikit-learn default hyper parameters.
- RT_2, same as RT_1, but with a tree depth of 6 (equal or better performance than LM_1).
- RT_3, same as RT_1, but with a tree depth of 10 (equal or better performance than LM_2).
- RT_4, same as RT_1, but with a tree depth of 11 (equal or better performance than Keytel's regression equation with VO_{2max} (K_1).
- RT_5, same as RT_1, but with a tree depth of 12 (a deeper tree would exceed the available memory on the PineTime smartwatch).
- RT_6, same as RT_4, but with VO_{2max} as additional feature

As can be seen in Figure 1, a tree depth of more than 20 does not lead to a smaller mean absolute error. Furthermore it becomes visible that at a tree depth of approx. 15, errors obtained with the test data set begin to differ slightly from those obtained with the training data set, which could be a possible indication for over-training.

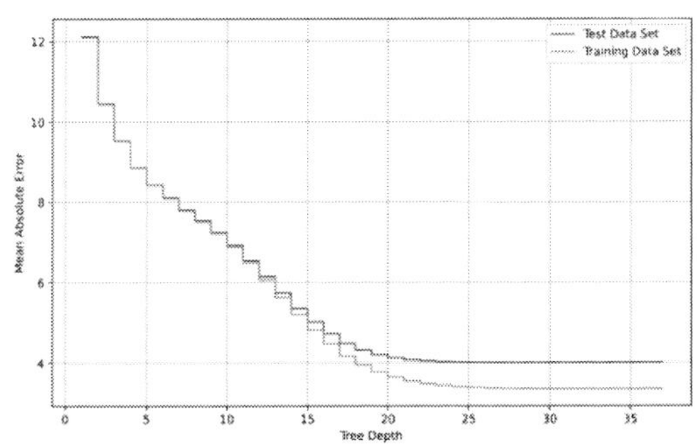

Figure 1. Tree depth vs. mean absolute error.

Along the same lines as with regression trees, we first trained a random forest with default parameters, resulting in a promising performance, yet unmanageable code size for the PineTime smartwatch:

- RF_1: Random forest with scikit-learn default parameters; heart rate, age, weight, and gender.
- RF_2: same as RF_1, tree depth of 6, 10 trees.
- RF_2: same as RF_1, tree depth of 9, 10 trees.

C. Code Generation and Deployment

After the models had been trained using the scikit-learn library inside a Python environment, we used m2cgen to create C code which we then cross-compiled for the C++-based InfiniTime operating system [21] (version 1.8.0) running on the PineTime smartwatch. For regression trees and random forests, m2cgen generates a function `double score(double* input)` which contains sequences of hard-coded if/else statements, therefore just consuming ROM and only little RAM.

Similiar to Sudharsan et al. [22], in an effort to reduce memory demands, all double keywords and as double literals were substituted in the generated code using regular expressions, furthermore instead of floating point numbers, we employed fixed point arithmetic numbers by multiplying with a factor of 1000, resulting in the overall use of integer numbers.

The InfiniTime OS is based on FreeRTOS and therefore employs multiple tasks, one of which is responsible for performing heart rate measurements. We therefore extended the `void HeartRateTask::Work()` method so that whenever a heart rate measurement is available, the `score()` function containing the code for the regressor is called to predict EE. As suggested by [21], we make use of puncover [23] to analyze the mapfile written by the C/C++ compiler (ARM-GCC, version 9-2020-q2-update) and determine the amount of ROM and RAM required by each regressor.

Due to the generous amount of memory, the Apple Watch is capable of running more complex models with more memory available to them. We therefore deployed RT_1 and RF_1 on the Apple Watch. The two regressors were trained using the same Python code as for the PineTime. The m2cgen code generation utility is not necessary, since the watch is programmable directly in Swift and can also use the trained models as resource files. The models need to be converted however, this is achieved using Apple's Core ML Tools library [24] [25]. The conversion is from a scikit-learn (version 0.19.2) trained model to a mlmodel file, which can then be easily integrated. In contrast to the PineTime, where code is executed in place, on the Apple Watch, once the app is executed, the model code runs in RAM to make predictions.

For a detailed analysis of the memory usage on the Apple Watch we used *Instruments* (version 13.0) as another tool inside the Xcode bundle (version 13.1) with which information can be collected regarding but not limited to memory leaks, time profiling, memory allocation statistics etc. We documented the amount of heap memory that was allocated by the watch application needed to perform a prediction, as well as the entire application size.

IV. Results and Discussion

Figure 4 compares the determined coefficients of determination. Our linear regression model LM_1 ($EE = -122.52022356 + 0.53176246hr + 0.26039323a + 0.23666578m + 0.39951689h - 7.88144777g$) is on par with Keytel's second equation (R^2 of 0.735 vs. 0.737) and also LM_2 ($EE = -103.97232241 + 0.54302212hr + 0.34344245a + 0.08775421m + 0.10690366h - 0.14505558g + 0.01021273o$) which perform quite similar (R^2 of 0.805 vs. 0.821) (EE: energy expenditure in KJ; hr: heart rate in beats/minute; a: age in years; m: body mass in kg; h: height in cm; g: gender (0 = male, 1 = female); o: VO_{2max} in ml/kg/min). Also the regression equation with basic parameters (e.g., age, height, mass, bodymass index (BMI), age-predicted HR_{max}) by Charlot et al. [12] ($R^2 = 0.809$) is similar; however, they use resting heart rate as an additional feature.

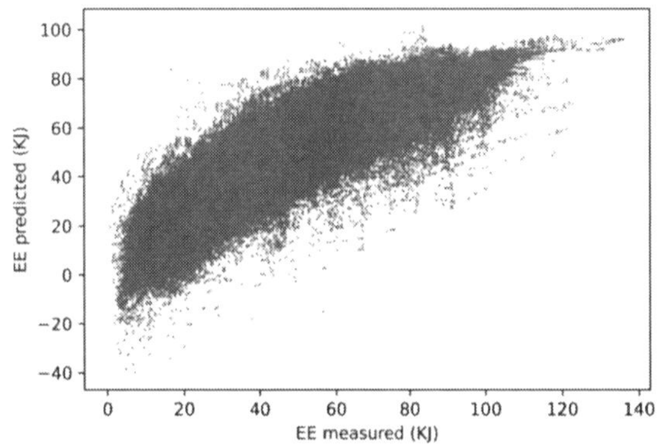

Figure 2. EE vs. predicted EE by LM_2.

RT_2, a regression tree with a depth of 6 exhibits $R^2 = 0.748$ which is similar to Keytel's equation without VO_{2max}.

RT_3 with a tree depth of 10 is comparable to LM_2. A tree size of 11 leads to a coefficient of determination of 0.825 which is almost the same as Keytel's equation K_1. However, both regression trees do not use VO_{2max} and perform the same as linear regression models, they are of particular interest to amateur athletes who do not know their VO_{2max}. Finally, increasing tree depth to 12 leads to $R^2 = 0.840$, which is better than Keytel's first equation, again without using VO_{2max}. Incorporating VO_{2max} into a tree of depth 11 gives an even higher coefficient ($R^2 = 0.877$).

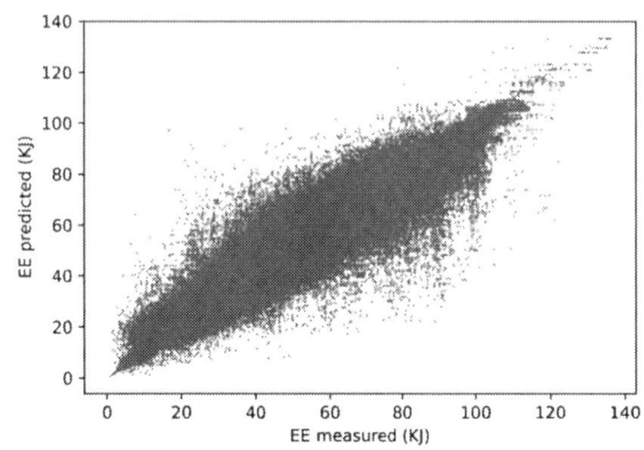

Figure 3. EE vs. predicted EE by DT_1.

The scatter plot in Figure 2 indicates that the linear model underestimates EE for submaximal and maximal efforts and can result in negative values near resting heart rate – something that is better taken care of by the regression tree model (see Figure 3).

Random forest models, which are also less prone to overfitting, perform best. However, for the PineTime smartwatch the biggest model we could accommodate had a maximum tree depth of 6 and used 10 estimators which led to a coefficient of (R^2 = 0.800) which is comparable to RT_3, again with the benefit of not using VO_{2max}. Increasing the number of estimators or tree depth then exceeded the available memory.

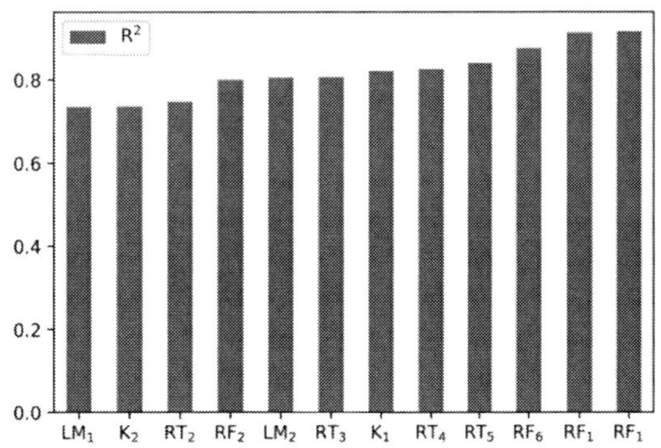

Figure 4. Coefficients of determination.

Table II summarizes the obtained regressor performances, as well as memory needs on the PineTime and Apple Watch. Despite performing more favorably than the linear models, tree-based regressors need more memory. Without any regressor, the code size needed for the heart rate task is 402 Bytes, the rest of the InfiniTime OS occupies 397434 Bytes, which means that 80.9 % of the available flash memory is used (only 480 KiB are available for applications). For the comparisons on the PineTime we used a release build environment, whereas a debug build environment was used for the Apple Watch. On the Apple Watch, the memory needed to hold the tree-based models is around 5.5 MiB, and the size of the application occupies approx. 20 MiB on the nonvolatile storage.

TABLE II
PERFORMANCE AND MEMORY REQUIREMENTS – PINETIME (PT) AND APPLE WATCH (AW).

Model	R^2	*MAE*	*PT ROM (Bytes)*	*PT Flash %*	*AW Model MiB*	*AW Size (MiB)*
LM_1	0.735	8.43	456	81.0	–	–
LM_2	0.805	7.26	446	81.0	–	–
RT_1	0.914	3.51	–	–	5.54	19.3
RT_2	0.748	8.09	1222	81.1	–	–
RT_3	0.807	6.87	14970	83.9	–	–
RT_4	0.825	6.49	28732	86.7	–	–
RT_5	0.840	6.10	54194	91.9	–	–
RT_5	0.877	5.33	30912	87.2	–	–
RF_1	0.917	3.53	–	–	5.21	19.8
RF_2	0.800	7.06	65576	94.2	–	–

V. CONCLUSIONS AND FUTURE WORK

In this paper, we described how to estimate energy expenditure from heart rate with a higher coefficient of determination using tree-based regressors than commonly used linear models. Using data from 892 graded exercise tests we trained various models and selected one which not only performed better than the linear model but also fitted in the flash memory of the open source smartwach PineTime. Our tree-based model does not need to know VO_{2max} but achieves a comparable result as the linear model with VO_{2max} making it especially interesting for amateur athletes. The additional memory on the PineTime smartwach needed to store the tree increased the the original firmware size of 390 KiB to 416 KiB. If VO_{2max} is available, then a tree with a depth of 11 achieves a coefficient of 0.877, and the total memory size is 418 KiB.

When considering the Apple Watch as another amateur athlete tool the memory constraint becomes irrelevant, since the regressors used in this paper can be utilized on the watch with no difficulty and result in an acceptable memory usage of less than 10 MiB.

In contrast to the linear model, our regression tree-based model seems to predict EE for sub-maximal, maximal and light efforts better. However, this still needs to be further investigated by defining limits of agreement and performing an ANOVA. Because the database contains data from treadmill tests only, it is not possible to validate how our model performs in other contexts, e.g., cycling or nordic walking. Consequently, we plan to extend the database in the future.

REFERENCES

[1] A. P. Hills, N. Mokhtar, and N. M. Byrne, "Assessment of physical activity and energy expenditure: An overview of objective measures," *Frontiers in Nutrition*, vol. 1, 2014. [Online]. Available: https://www.frontiersin.org/article/10.3389/fnut.2014.00005

[2] I.-M. Lee, C. cheng Hsieh, and R. S. Paffenbarger, "Exercise Intensity and Longevity in Men: The Harvard Alumni Health Study," *JAMA*, vol. 273, no. 15, pp. 1179–1184, 04 1995.

[3] J. Morris, J. Heady, P. Raffle, C. Roberts, and J. Parks, "Coronary heart-disease and physical activity of work," *The Lancet*, vol. 262, no. 6795, pp. 1053–1057, 1953.

[4] G. D. Batty and I.-M. Lee, "Physical activity and coronary heart disease." *BMJ (Clinical research ed.)*, vol. 328, no. 7448, pp. 1089–1090, 2004.

[5] K. Domaszewska, M. Boraczynski, Y.-Y. Tang, J. Gronek, K. Wochna, T. Boraczynski, D. Wielinski, and P. Gronek], "Protective effects of exercise become especially important for the aging immune system in the covid-19 era," *Aging and disease*, vol. 13, no. 1, pp. 129–143, 2022.

[6] D. Fister, I. Fister, S. Rauter, and I. Fister, "Generating eating plans for athletes using the particle swarm optimization," in *2016 IEEE 17th International Symposium on Computational Intelligence and Informatics (CINTI)*, 2016, pp. 000 193–000 198.

[7] J. Rivera, A. McPherson, J. Hamilton, C. Birken, M. Coons, S. Iyer, A. Agarwal, C. Lalloo, and J. Stinson, "Mobile apps for weight management: A scoping review," *JMIR Mhealth Uhealth*, vol. 4, no. 3, p. e87, Jul 2016.

[8] S. S. Coughlin, "Use of consumer wearable devices to promote physical activity: A review of health intervention studies," *Journal of Environment and Health Sciences*, vol. 2, pp. 1– 6, 2016.

[9] D. Ndahimana and K. Eun-Kyung, "Measurement methods for physical activity and energy expenditure: a review." *Clinical nutrition research*, vol. 6, no. 2, pp. 68–80, 2017.

[10] W. Leonard, "Measuring human energy expenditure: what have we learned from the flex-heart rate method?" *American journal of human biology : the official journal of the Human Biology Council*, vol. 15, pp. 479–89, 07 2003.

[11] L. Keytel, J. Goedecke, T. Noakes, H. Hiiloskorpi, R. Laukkanen, L. van der Merwe, and E. Lambert, "Prediction of energy expenditure from heart rate monitoring during submaximal exercise," *Journal of sports sciences*, vol. 23, pp. 289–97, 04 2005.
[12] K. Charlot, J. Cornolo, R. Borne, J. Brugniaux, J.-P. Richalet, D. Chapelot, and A. Pichon, "Improvement of energy expenditure prediction from heart rate during running," *Physiological measurement*, vol. 35, pp. 253–266, 01 2014.
[13] K. Ellis, J. Kerr, S. Godbole, G. R. G. Lanckriet, D. Wing, and S. J. Marshall, "A random forest classifier for the prediction of energy expenditure and type of physical activity from wrist and hip accelerometers." *Physiological measurement*, vol. 35 11, pp. 2191–203, 2014.
[14] F. Pedregosa, G. Varoquaux, A. Gramfort, V. Michel, B. Thirion, O. Grisel, M. Blondel, P. Prettenhofer, R. Weiss, V. Dubourg, J. Vanderplas, A. Passos, D. Cournapeau, M. Brucher, M. Perrot, and E. Duchesnay, "Scikit-learn: Machine learning in Python," *Journal of Machine Learning Research*, vol. 12, pp. 2825–2830, 2011.
[15] "m2cgen (model 2 code generator)," 2022, URL: https://github.com/BayesWitnesses/m2cgen [accessed: 2022-4-1].
[16] "Pinetime)," 2022, URL: https://wiki.pine64.org/wiki/PineTime [accessed: 2022-4-1].
[17] D. Mongin, J. García-Romero, and J. R. Alvero-Cruz, "Treadmill maximal exercise tests from the exercise physiology and human performance lab of the university of malaga (version 1.0.1)," PhysionNet, 2021, URL: https://doi.org/10.1080/15438627.2021.1954513 [accessed: 2022-4-1].
[18] D. Mongin, C. Chabert, D. S. Courvoisier, J. García-Romero, and J. R. Alvero-Cruz, "Heart rate recovery to assess fitness: comparison of different calculation methods in a large cross-sectional study," *Research in Sports Medicine*, vol. 0, no. 0, pp. 1–14, 2021.
[19] A. L. Goldberger, L. A. N. Amaral, L. Glass, J. M. Hausdorff, P. C. Ivanov, R. G. Mark, J. E. Mietus, G. B. Moody, C.-K. Peng, and H. E. Stanley, "PhysioBank, PhysioToolkit, and PhysioNet: Components of a new research resource for complex physiologic signals," *Circulation*, vol. 101, no. 23, pp. e215–e220, 2000 (June 13).
[20] J. B. d. V. Weir, "New methods for calculating metabolic rate with special reference to protein metabolism," *The Journal of Physiology*, vol. 109, no. 1-2, pp. 1–9, 1949.
[21] "Infinitime," 2022, URL: https://infinitime.io/ [accessed: 2022-4-1].
[22] B. Sudharsan, P. Patel, J. G. Breslin, and M. I. Ali, "Ultra-fast machine learning classifier execution on iot devices without sram consumption," in *2021 IEEE International Conference on Pervasive Computing and Communications Workshops and other Affiliated Events (PerCom Workshops)*, 2021, pp. 316–319.
[23] "puncover," 2022, URL: https://github.com/HBehrens/puncover [accessed: 2022-4-1].
[24] "coremltools," 2017, URL: https://github.com/apple/coremltools [accessed: 2022-4-1].
[25] "coremltools documentation," 2017, URL: https://coremltools.readme.io/docs [accessed: 2022-4-1].

Context-Aware Security Intelligence of Vulnerability Scanners in Cloud-native Environments

Simon Ammer, Jens Krösche
Mobility & Energy
University of Applied Sciences Upper Austria
Hagenberg im Mühlkreis, Austria
email: firstname.lastname@fh-hagenberg.at

Markus Gierlinger, Mario Kahlhofer
Dynatrace Research
Linz, Austria
email: firstname.lastname@dynatrace.com

***Abstract*—Even as black-box web vulnerability scanners help identify security vulnerabilities of web applications, they still have problems with false alarms, as they lack insight into the context of applications. Without this supplemental information like the topology of the underlying application or the runtime, scanners cannot precisely assess a threat's actual severity, leading to false alarms and a challenge for security experts to prioritize vulnerabilities. Especially with the increasing popularity of microservices and highly dynamic cloud environments, this prioritization task becomes more difficult due to this environment. This paper bridges this gap by enriching web vulnerability scanner reports with context information to understand security threats better and reduce false positives. To this end, we developed a rule-based system that is extensible for multiple use cases, and we propose a framework to evaluate the approach's effectiveness using the insecure web applications Unguard and Open Web Application Security Project (OWASP) JuiceShop.**

***Keywords*—cloud computing; web application security; distributed systems security; context-awareness; rule-based adaptation.**

I. Introduction

Cloud computing is a fundamental building block for today's digital transformation, and a cloud-first strategy is becoming the norm, according to Taleb and Mohamed [1]. However, according to Behl [2], cloud computing also adds new risks of being vulnerable to cyber-attacks and demands more than traditional security solutions. Even as cloud providers ensure security on a certain level based on the shared responsibility model like the ones from Amazon [3] and Microsoft [4], still, according to the models, the customers also have security responsibilities depending on the service model. Several methods exist to improve security. The Amazon Web Services (AWS) DevSecOps reference architecture from Manepalli [5] of AWS and also the DevSecOps primitives for a reference platform from Chandramouli [6] of the National Institute of Standards and Technology (NIST) list the following methods:

- Software Composition Analysis (SCA): Identify potential risks when using third-party software (i.e., libraries, packages, etc.).
- Static Application Security Testing (SAST): Analyze the source code during development to find issues.
- Dynamic Application Security Testing (DAST): Examine the outside security posture.
- Interactive Application Security Testing (IAST): Combine the working principle of SAST and DAST.
- Runtime Application Self Protection (RASP): Monitor applications in run-time to detect threats and block some execution paths if necessary.

Dynamic web application vulnerability scanners are in the category of DAST tools. These tools need minimal human interaction and have the advantage that they are programming language independent. Especially, the automatic aspect is vital with the growing number of web applications where penetration tests are limited due to resource and time constraints. Such tools can also support the DevSecOps approach of companies by running security scans automatically in a continuous integration and delivery (CI/CD) pipeline before releasing applications. The scanners themselves search for vulnerabilities by attacking and probing the application's web and API interfaces from an outside perspective.

Offered scanners also report false positives according to Bau, Bursztein, Gupta, *et al.* [7] and Alsaleh, Alomar, Alshreef, *et al.* [8], which adds to the challenge of security experts to prioritize vulnerabilities correctly. For example, false-positive Structured Query Language (SQL) injections where the detected technology does not match the actual technology. Some research, exemplified in Section II, tries to create new scanners that provide better results, whereas others emphasize techniques that combine static and dynamic security testing elements. The higher complexity of modern web applications and microservice architectures make this undertaking even more challenging because they use different technologies at different abstraction layers. Also, with the ever-changing nature of cloud environments, the prioritization of vulnerabilities for security experts becomes even more complex.

This work proposes a technique to support this prioritization and reduce false positives of security tools in a cloud-native environment by utilizing inherent contextual information of the environment, like topology and runtime. The proposed method is generally applicable, but the implemented prototype focuses on the open-source web application security scanner OWASP Zed Attack Proxy (ZAP), utilizes Kubernetes as container orchestration service, and uses Dynatrace as an observability software. However, other observability platforms can also be

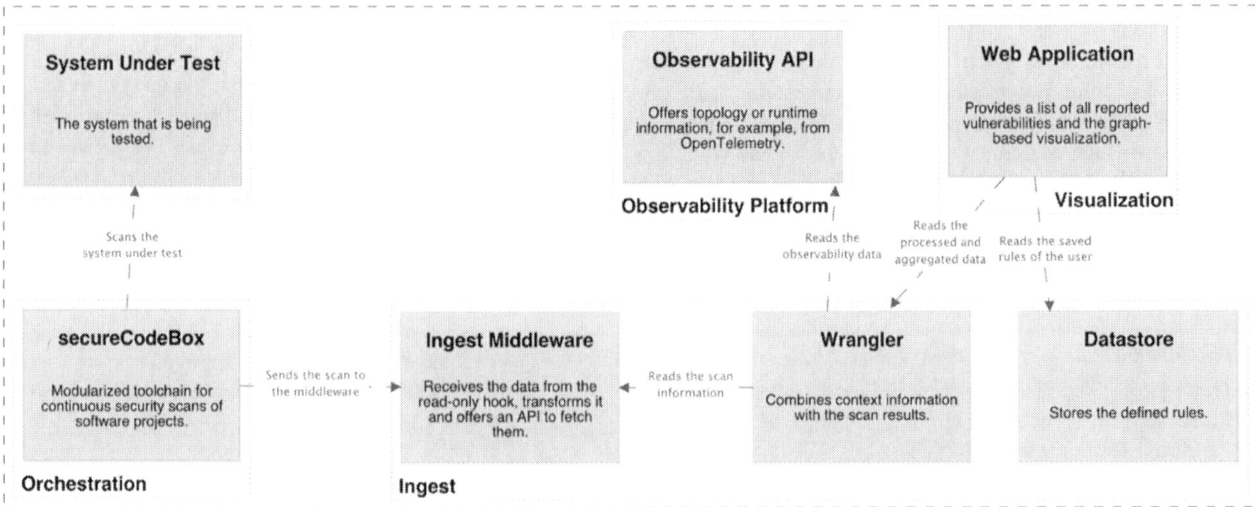

Fig. 1. The proposed architecture of the system.

used if they offer data like the expected data structure shown in Section III.

Specifically, our contributions are:

- *Context-aware ruleset engine*: DAST is known to report false-positive alerts according to Doupé, Cova, and Vigna [9]. A context-aware rule-based filtering supports the prioritization of threats and the reduction of false-positives.
- *Graph-based security posture visualization*: The method of visualizing the relationship between application assets and topology information from an attacker's perspective. This visualization assists security experts in prioritizing threats.

Second, we propose a framework to evaluate the methods using the insecure web application Unguard (not public at the time of this writing) and OWASP JuiceShop.

The rest of the work is organized as follows. Section II discusses related work. The proposed concept is described in Section III. Section IV presents a framework to evaluate the approach with two insecure web applications. Finally, in Section V, we summarize and discuss, and give an outlook for future work.

II. Related Work

As proposed to Doupé, Cova, and Vigna [9], web application scanners are comprised of three modules in most cases: a crawler, an attacker, and an analysis module. The crawler tries to find all the reachable pages and input points of an application by following redirects and links. The attacker module then uses the result to generate values that may trigger a vulnerability. As last step, the analysis module analyzes the application's responses to detect vulnerabilities. A systematic review by Seng, Ithnin, and Said [10] analyzed the methodology of existing academic manuscripts for quantifying scanners' quality and found no standard methods. Only a common practice, namely calculating the number of detected vulnerabilities, was found. Mburano and Si [11] used additional metrics like the True Positive Rate (TPR) and False Positive Rate (FPR) and carried out a benchmark of open-source scanner results using the Open Web Application Security Project (OWASP) Benchmark and the Web Application Vulnerability Scanner Evaluation Project (WAVSEP).

Studies from 2010 of Bau, Bursztein, Gupta, *et al.* [7] and Doupé, Cova, and Vigna [9] show that scanners offer good results for simple historical vulnerabilities but have difficulties with advanced or second-order forms. Another finding was that the cost of a scanner and the provided functionality have no strong correlation. False positives occurred due to the disclosure of server paths and absolute paths of anchors, but there were also genuine ones. More recent studies provided similar results with Alsaleh, Alomar, Alshreef, *et al.* [8] recommending better verification checks of reported false positives of investigated open source scanners to simplify the manual verification process. Also, Anhar and Suryanto [12] state that further research is necessary for modern web applications based on frameworks like React, Angular, and similar ones.

According to Gartner [13], context-aware security (CAS) is described as the usage of additional contextual information to improve security decisions, which is used in our work. To the best of the authors' knowledge, there is not much research on web application scanners utilizing CAS. Even so, some work on intrusion detection systems (IDS) like the following relies on contextual information. Chergui and Boustia [14] list the following information for compromised entities as helpful: network configuration, protocols, operating system, services, and applications. The latter three are also used in the prototype of this work. Eschelbeck and Krieger [15] use a similar approach by including services, ports, operating systems, and vulnerabilities as information to eliminate noise from IDS.

III. Methodology

This paper utilizes the two chosen context information, topology and runtime, relying on the monitoring and observability platforms or systems to provide the necessary information. Such systems know about the topology of the applications but do not necessarily have access to the actual code. Therefore, SAST and IAST are not the focus of this work. The main focus is DAST because they attack an application from the outside and do not have run-time information which the observability platform can provide.

A. Architecture

Our system Themis, shown in Figure 1, consists of four main components. The *orchestration* automates the scheduling of security testing tools in Kubernetes. The *observability platform* collects all contextual information. The *ingest* fuses data and integrates multiple data sources afterwards, and the *visualization* displays the information for security experts.

1) Orchestration: Runs different security scans, either on demand or in a specified interval. It also extracts the scan result and parses it to a unified format finding format of the secureCodeBox project [16]. Afterwards, the data is sent to the receiving *ingest* components using a webhook.

2) Observability Platform: The observability platform has constant 'insight' into the applications and collects the monitored data, for example, from OpenTelemetry. Listing 2 shows the expected data structure of such an observability platform as a JavaScript Object Notation (JSON) object. The attributes $toRelationships$ and $fromRelationships$ contain the connections of an application to others. The $softwareTechnologies$ attribute shows the application's technologies like C# and Java.

```
[{
  "hostname": "jshop.juiceshop.svc",
  "toRelationships": {
    "calls": [
      "APPLICATION-C46735D64G092C8H"
    ]
  },
  "softwareTechnologies": [{
      "type": "NODE_JS (14.18)"
  }],
  "fromRelationships": {
    "runsOn": [
      "PROCESS_GROUP-FQVDC6732B412233"
    ]
  }
}]
```

Fig. 2. Data structure for the topology and runtime information.

3) Ingest: The core part of this work, the ingest, is split into three parts: Middleware, Wrangler, and Datastore. The first part, the Ingest Middleware, transforms the result of the orchestration component and potential external vulnerability scanners to the DAST report format of Gitlab [17], partially seen in Figure 3. The Wrangler then uses this report to correlate the results with the data of the observability platform. The correlation is performed based on the hostname of the application, which is present both in the topology data and the scan result. The aggregated data can then be used to filter the scan results with pre- and user-defined rules, which are saved in the Datastore. Security experts manually create these rules, but the architecture could be used to enable problem-specific rule sets automatically based on specific characteristics of applications in further work.

```
"vulnerabilities": [{
  "name": "SQL Injection - SQLite",
  "identifiers": [{ "name": "CWE-89" }],
  "severity": "HIGH",
  "location": {
    "hostname": "http://jshop.juiceshop.svc",
  }
}]
```

Fig. 3. Data structure for the found vulnerabilities of a scan result.

4) Visualization: A penetration tester can view the ingested data on a web application. Furthermore, it has a rule editor for custom user rules defined in Rego [18], a query language inspired by Datalog. A sample rule is shown in Listing 4 that filters the false-positive SQL injections, mentioned in Section I, where the detected technology does not match the actual technology. For example, possible injection of MySQL, while the application itself does not use this technology.

```
deny[msg] {
  input.vulnerability.type == "SQLi"
  not input.vulnerability.technology == \
      topology.database.type
  msg: sprintf("SQLi vulnerability %s does \
      not match the underlying database.")
}
```

Fig. 4. A user-defined rule to avoid false positives of SQL injection alerts.

IV. Discussion

Previous research from Seng, Ithnin, and Said [10] and Doupé, Cova, and Vigna [9] shows that quantifying the results of web application security scanners is complex and common practice is to run the scanner against multiple testbeds. One important metric is the TPR of discovered vulnerabilities of such tests. As this paper does not improve the internals of web application security scanners but aims to improve the produced results by reducing false positives, spurious vulnerabilities are the most important metric. This section outlines the used methods for evaluating the proposed technique.

The proposed approach is evaluated by running one open-source (OWASP ZAP) and one commercial scanner (Tenable Web App Scanning), against two web applications. One of these testbeds is the monolith application OWASP JuiceShop, which includes real-world applications' security flaws and vulnerabilities from the OWASP TopTen. The second insecure application is a custom testbed called Unguard from the company Dynatrace that contains hand-inserted vulnerabilities with proven attack patterns. These two applications have different application architectures to analyse which contextual information is helpful in which architecture.

False Positives: Whether the false positive rate improved with the proposed approach still needs to be evaluated. Nevertheless, it is assumed that the results with Unguard will be better than the ones with OWASP JuiceShop. Because the latter application is a monolith, the topology does not provide much value here. Only the information of the application's technology will therefore be beneficial for the results, which will result in a worse filter result.

Visualization: The graph-based visualization of the context seems to provide value in the mitigation process. Still, this result is hard to measure as it is subjective based on the application's user. Nevertheless, it is shown that vulnerability and topology information can also be merged and presented graphically.

V. Conclusion

In this paper, we presented a system that tries to reduce false positives of scanners in a cloud environment. Although there is much research on improving the functionality of web application scanners, utilizing contextual information is not much examined to the authors' knowledge. To this end, an architecture to combine scanner results and topology information has been proposed, and a prototype called Themis with a rule-based filtering approach and graph-based visualization of found vulnerabilities was shown. The effectiveness will be thoroughly evaluated in the near future with the two projects, Unguard and OWASP JuiceShop, using the FPR as a metric. It is assumed that results with OWASP JuiceShop will be restricted due to the monolithic architecture of the application. Better results are expected for microservice-based applications where topology information is beneficial. Additionally, the effectiveness of the rule-based filtering and the graph-based visualization's helpfulness for security experts has to be further evaluated in a production environment.

Acknowledgment

This research was partially supported by Dynatrace. We thank our colleagues from the Cloud Application Security Protection department.

References

[1] N. Taleb and E. A. Mohamed, "Cloud Computing Trends: A Literature Review," Jan. 16, 2020. DOI: 10.36941/ajis-2020-0008.

[2] A. Behl, "Emerging Security Challenges in Cloud Computing: An Insight to Cloud Security Challenges and their Mitigation," in *2011 World Congress on Information and Communication Technologies*, Dec. 2011, pp. 217–222. DOI: 10.1109/WICT.2011.6141247.

[3] Amazon. (Apr. 2022). Shared Responsibility Model, Amazon Web Services, Inc., [Online]. Available: https://aws.amazon.com/compliance/shared-responsibility-model/ (visited on 04/04/2022).

[4] Microsoft. (Mar. 1, 2022). Shared Responsibility in the Cloud, [Online]. Available: https://docs.microsoft.com/en-us/azure/security/fundamentals/shared-responsibility (visited on 04/04/2022).

[5] S. Manepalli. (Jun. 25, 2021). Building an End-to-end Kubernetes-based DevSecOps Software Factory on AWS, Amazon Web Services, [Online]. Available: https://aws.amazon.com/blogs/devops/building-an-end-to-end-kubernetes-based-devsecops-software-factory-on-aws/ (visited on 04/04/2022).

[6] R. Chandramouli, "Implementation of DevSecOps for A Microservices-based Application with Service Mesh," Sep. 29, 2021. DOI: 10.6028/NIST.SP.800-204C.

[7] J. Bau, E. Bursztein, D. Gupta, and J. Mitchell, "State of the Art: Automated Black-Box Web Application Vulnerability Testing," in *2010 IEEE Symposium on Security and Privacy*, Oakland, CA, USA: IEEE, May 2010, pp. 332–345. DOI: 10.1109/SP.2010.27.

[8] M. Alsaleh, N. Alomar, M. Alshreef, A. Alarifi, and A. Al-Salman, "Performance-Based Comparative Assessment of Open Source Web Vulnerability Scanners," *Security and Communication Networks*, vol. 2017, pp. 1–14, May 24, 2017. DOI: 10.1155/2017/6158107.

[9] A. Doupé, M. Cova, and G. Vigna, "Why Johnny Can't Pentest: An Analysis of Black-Box Web Vulnerability Scanners," in *Detection of Intrusions and Malware, and Vulnerability Assessment*, C. Kreibich and M. Jahnke, Eds., vol. 6201, Bonn, Germany: Springer, Jul. 8, 2010, pp. 111–131. DOI: 10.1007/978-3-642-14215-4_7.

[10] L. Seng, N. Ithnin, and S. Said, "The Approaches to quantify Web Application Security Scanners Quality: A Review," *International Journal of Advanced Computer Research*, vol. 8, pp. 285–312, Sep. 28, 2018. DOI: 10.19101/IJACR.2018.838012.

[11] B. Mburano and W. Si, "Evaluation of Web Vulnerability Scanners Based on OWASP Benchmark," in *2018 26th International Conference on Systems Engineering (ICSEng)*, Sydney, NSW, Australia: IEEE, Dec. 2018, pp. 1–6. DOI: 10.1109/ICSENG.2018.8638176.

[12] A. A. Anhar and Y. Suryanto, "Evaluation of Web Application Vulnerability Scanner for Modern Web Application," presented at the International Conference on Artificial Intelligence and Computer Science Technology, Yogyakarta, Indonesia: IEEE, 2021, pp. 200–204. DOI: 10.1109/ICAICST53116.2021.9497831.

[13] Gartner. (Apr. 2022). Definition of Context-aware Security, Gartner, [Online]. Available: https://www.gartner.com/en/information-technology/glossary/context-aware-security (visited on 04/04/2022).

[14] N. Chergui and N. Boustia, "Contextual-based Approach to reduce False Positives," *IET Information Security*, vol. 14, no. 1, pp. 89–98, 2020. DOI: 10.1049/iet-ifs.2018.5479.

[15] G. Eschelbeck and M. Krieger, "Eliminating Noise from Intrusion Detection Systems," *Information Security Technical Report*, vol. 8, no. 4, pp. 26–33, Apr. 1, 2003. DOI: 10.1016/S1363-4127(03)00004-9.

[16] secureCodeBox. (Apr. 2022). Finding Format, Finding, [Online]. Available: https://docs.securecodebox.io/docs/api/finding (visited on 04/04/2022).

[17] Gitlab. (Mar. 29, 2022). DAST Report Format, GitLab, [Online]. Available: https://gitlab.com/gitlab-org/security-products/security-report-schemas/-/blob/master/dist/dast-report-format.json (visited on 04/04/2022).

[18] Open Policy Agent. (Apr. 2022). Policy Language - Rego, Open Policy Agent, [Online]. Available: https://openpolicyagent.org/docs/latest/policy-language/ (visited on 04/04/2022).

Complex Responsive Processes in a Multi-Agent System: A Knowledge Accelerator

Knowledge Sharing in a Self-Adaptive Multi-Agent System based on the principles of Complex Responsive Processes of Relating

Guido T. H. J. Willemsen
ISCTE-IUL/ISTA
University Institute of Lisbon
Lisbon, Portugal
Email: gwnou@iscte-iul.pt

Luis M. P. Correia
Dept. Informática, LASIGE, Faculdade de Ciências,
Universidade de Lisboa
Lisbon, Portugal
Email: luis.correia@ciencias.ulisboa.pt

Marco A. Janssen
School of Sustainability / School of Complex Adaptive Systems
Arizona State University
Phoenix, USA
Email: marco.janssen@asu.edu

Abstract—**Complex Responsive Processes (CRP) focus on the interaction between agents, where they exchange knowledge, opinions, experience, and values. In decentralized decision making, this could accelerate the monitoring, analysis, planning and execution process, as defined in a control mechanism like MAPE-K. For Multi-Agent Systems with a decentralized or hybrid architecture the gesture (e.g., agent *expression*) and response dynamics of complex responsive interaction could be valuable to reduce the entropy of a system. Until today, the CRP mechanisms have not been formalized in Multi-Agent decentralized decision making as it lacks a formal model to express inter-agent dialectics. This position paper discloses the area where an extension of the MAPE-K control cycle can be made to include the formalized CRP processes. This extension consists of a set of methods that include the responsive processes of multiple agents and will be used to update the Knowledge base in the MAPE-K model.**

Keywords: Complex Responsive Processes of Relating; MAPE-K; Multi-Agent Systems; Complex Adaptive Systems; Beer Game.

I. INTRODUCTION

In the summer of 1988, the premium beer producer Heineken launched a promising new alcohol-free beer called *Buckler*. After an initial successful market entrance, the sales figures were dropping dramatically since January 1990 and there was a very clear reason why this happened. In a live TV show on New Year's Eve 1989, a famous Dutch comedian claimed that Buckler consumers were "losers" and lack masculinity. Nobody could imagine that this single statement could result in a tremendous loss of market share and even a premature exit of the brand in the Dutch market. The "Buckler-effect" has become a worst-case practice marketing case on Dutch business schools [1].

Demand and supply in logistics are difficult to align as temporal and spatial differences should be bridged. Traditionally, forecasting and planning techniques were powerful mechanisms to control the logistic chain, to bring demand and supply together in the most efficient way [2]. However, situations like the Buckler-effect, or recently the blockage of the Suez Canal by the *Ever-Given* shows that the external factors can suddenly impact the behavior of market players and will have a critical role in decision-making [3].

A marketplace is a place where cooperation or collaboration and competition of players result in dynamic behavior [4][5], which can be characterized as a Complex Adaptive System (CAS) [6] and where Complex Responsive Processes (CRP) [7] occur. The emergent behavior that results from cooperation is difficult to control, and the non-linear characteristics will make predictions about the players' behavior difficult [8], even when information is shared throughout the supply chain. Recently, the use of Multi-Agent Systems (MAS) has gained improved insight in complex behavior in decentralized decision making in logistic processes. However, current models in decentralized, multi-agent collaborative decision processes within supply chains are still not efficient, precise and lead to poor operability [9]. Research in the field of Supply Chain Networks is promising when traditional supply chains are conceptualized as CAS [10]. To achieve a better alignment of demand and supply, more advanced techniques are required, which take the emergent characteristics of the market into account, like the bull-whip effect or social influencing [11]-[13]. The impact of gesture and response dynamics in multi-agent knowledge exchange is lacking at the moment.

In this paper the rationale for research is elaborated, followed by a description of related work. After that, the Multi-Agent Control Cycle structure is clarified and the extended control cycle mechanism will be described. This will be the foundation for a possible further extension of the model into Complex Responsive Processes.

II. Rationale for Research

In multi-agent knowledge creation, each single agent will update its Knowledge Base (KB), for each cycle in runtime. Process patterns, data analysis algorithms, system data or environmental data can be stored in its own knowledge base. This knowledge will then be available for individual agent analysis and decisions. Decentralized decision making in Multi-Agent Systems is a useful resource to challenge complexity. Theories of knowledge sharing in Multi-Agent Systems still lack the emergent behavior of collaborating agents, more specifically the dynamics of the group in open Multi-Agent systems [60]. What happens when we add the exchange of knowledge and dialectics between agents based on trust and group logic to a Multi-Agent System? Or in other words, what is the role of Complex Responsive Processes in a Self-Adapting Multi-Agent System with decentralized decision making? This area of multi-agent behavior needs to be investigated in more detail to understand the emergent characteristics of symbiotic relations between agents. This paper describes the area of research to extend the current Multi-Agent control cycles with dialectical relation between agents. To understand the dialectics between agents, a formal model should be developed that will describe the exchange of gesture and response to support decentralized decisions. The research should result in a clear extension of the MAPE-K model to facilitate the dialectic behavior between multiple agents.

III. Related Work

In the last decades, the digitization of markets and the availability of 'big data' enabled a quicker understanding of the space, in which economic decisions are made [14]. For companies to be successful, it has become critical to acquire knowledge from outside the organization [15]-[18], and to have the ability and strength to execute processes based on the capacities to interpret these data [18]-[21]. For companies, like the beer brewer mentioned earlier, the decisions to efficiently sell and distribute their bottles of beer to consumers should be heavily influenced by detailed understanding of their own capabilities and the information of the environment, in which they operate [22]. Recent developments in the knowledge of network dynamics, which can be applied to economic markets as complex systems [23], shows that not only the environment dictates how agents should act but also agents can influence the environment in their own favor [24]. At the same time, the dominant logic can be influenced by tight collaboration. Hence, as Banisch *et al.* [25] demonstrated, the logic of the dominating group could be challenged by the minority and even become the majority themselves, which has been described as the *Social Feedback Theory.* Critical for this domination is the strength of the agents in the group. The stronger the bonds between the agents, the higher the chance that they will become the majority. In economics, this has been labelled as the "bandwagon effect" [26].

Multi-Agent Systems with decentralized decision making can positively contribute to the added value of products and services in the supply chain [27] when they improve the degree of collaboration between them. From an architectural approach, an important principle for a resilient and adaptable supply chain network is *self-organization* [28]. Approaches for self-organization, defined as Self Adapting Systems (SAS), are described by Krupitzer *et al* [29], where a profound taxonomy is proposed. With this taxonomy, SASs are described in a few dimensions: time, level, reason, technique, and adaptation logic. According to Krupitzer *et al*, most approaches are reactive and exclude the impact of the action on its context, which requires further research on proactive and context-altering system architectures.

A recognized system for self-adaptation is the MAPE-K model [29]. Within MAPE-K the adaptation decision criteria are based on models, policies/rules, goals, or utilities. MAPE-K is a useful control model as it is formalized and supports multi-agent abstract state machines [61]. The control mechanisms in MAPE-K will be applied in a centralized, de-centralized or hybrid models. For MAS solutions, the decentralized model is appropriate to support self-adaptation [30]. An external implementation approach for the MAPE-K control loop, which is loosely coupled from the managed system, is superior in most cases [29]. Also, the adaptation decision criteria should be considered, based on models, policies/rules, goals, or utilities. Several models to exchange knowledge about the environment, system, goals and possibilities of adaptations between agents has been developed by Fisch *et al.* [31], where agents can learn from each other in a MAS setting. More work should be done on collaborative data mining and experience exchange.

When we focus on the collaboration between agents, it is important that all agents share the same language. In the last three decades, formal languages have been developed for MAS solutions. However, the acceptance level of MAS languages is still poor, as mainstream development platforms could to the job as well, with only small efforts. [32]. Nevertheless, several agent programming languages could improve the development of MASs and contain valuable concepts to use in MAS architectures. At the time, there is no MAS language that has been adopted as a de facto standard [32].

To be able to describe the formal model, the building blocks should be clarified: 1) MAPE-K model. 2) MAPE-K architecture, 3) Adaptation logic of the knowledge base and 4) The complex responsive processes of relating between agents.

IV. Multi-Agent Control Mechanisms

Multi-Agent Systems could be based on human or virtual agents, both capable of autonomous action and interaction with each other. As MAS is developing in the domain of Artificial Intelligence (AI), the semiosis of the human and virtual agents is gaining attention [33][34]. Formal theories of human intention, reasoning and decision making could be valuable to improve the mechanisms in a virtual MAS [35].

A. The MAPE-K model

To gain grip on organizational processes constituted of temporal actor behavior, control cycles are required [36]. These control cycles use knowledge of the environment and the internal state of the system to decide on the actions to be taken. In Multi-Agent Systems (MAS), the knowledge of the environment is embedded in the MAS architecture. A well-known control cycle process for MAS is MAPE-K. The MAPE-K architecture model structures the governance of a MAS system in five components, which constitute the control system. The environment is Monitored (M) and Analyzed (A), actions are Planned (P) and Executed (E). All these activities are based on an agent-specific Knowledge Base (K or KB) [37]. This KB includes data such as topology information, historical logs, metrics, symptoms, and policies, which are fed by the Monitoring component and updated by the Execution component. MAPE-K could be applied to several levels of the processes, both on a central and decentralized level. Decentralized control is managing the execution of the subsystem for each agent to achieve domain specific goals and will impact the environment [38] and shapes the behavior of higher-level processes. Centralized control on the other hand will take care of synchronization of these activities. Weyns *et al.* [39] describe several patterns for the interaction between centralized and decentralized control.

B. The Frameself Architecture for MAPE-K

The complexity of a distributed Multi-Agent System with MAPE-K control loops will lead to self-adaptation, -deployment and -configuration of information systems. This requires a clear architectural framework, on which agents will act and processes emerge. One of these architectures is the "Frameself" Architecture [40]. This architecture contains a fine-grained model of a MAPE-K loop, including related interfaces, where the environment is monitored, analyzed and changes are planned and implemented, based on an agent-specific knowledge base. As this architecture is fully integrated in the Unified Modelling Language (UML) it gives a clear approach for pragmatic solution. *Frameself* has been developed for Machine to Machine (M2M) behavior, but is suitable for use in a generic MAS context as well. The architecture fully embeds the MAPE-K loop and can be seen as a "mapping" solution from the theoretical to the pragmatic domain. The architecture consists of the five MAPE-K processes, Monitor, Analyze, Plan, Execute and Maintain Knowledge Base, which communicate via web services. The KB is used as a source for information sharing to facilitate process execution and decision making.

When autonomic systems use the MAPE-K architecture to decide in runtime, a detailed understanding is required about what, where, when, how, and with what tools data are collected from the environment. Hence, the way the data are dimensioned, classified, and translated should be clarified before a proper analysis can be done. When these data are analyzed, a suitable benchmark or expectation should be available to evaluate the performance of the system and applicability of business rules [41]. Based on this evaluation, the next operational process configuration is selected. The question raises if the existing rules and processes are appropriate for the state of the system in its context? This requires the need for a meta-adaptation layer, in which higher level evaluation, learning and verification is possible [42].

C. Monitoring

The monitoring process (Figure 1) consist of methods which will scan the environment on relevant events, aggregate, masks and normalize these and creates symptoms which will be send to the Analysis process. Often, these event handlers are also called *receptors*. All methods are managed by the Monitoring manager and knowledge is used from the KB or will be updated by the Knowledge Base Communicator (KBC). The methods used are identified as public (+) or private (-).

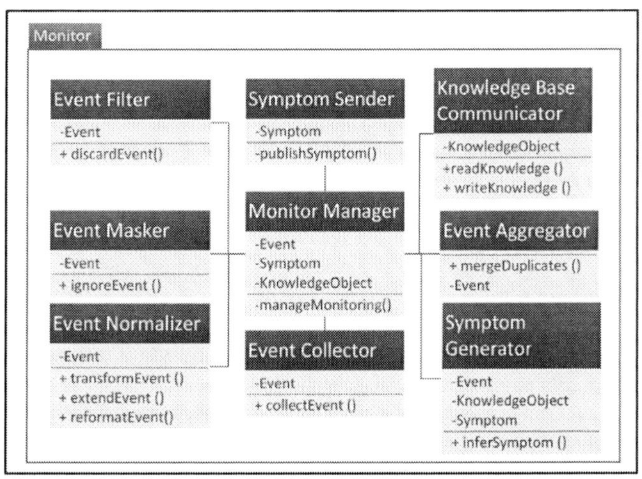

Figure 1. Frameself Monitoring Model.

D. Analysis

The symptom is received from the Monitoring process and a policy is validated and applied with separate methods. The Analysis phase (Figure 2) will take care of the evaluation of environmental phenomena and draw clear conclusions, based on policies. This will lead to the generation of a Request for Change (RfC), which is communicated to the Planner process. All knowledge about the policies is interfaced bi-directionally with the KB.

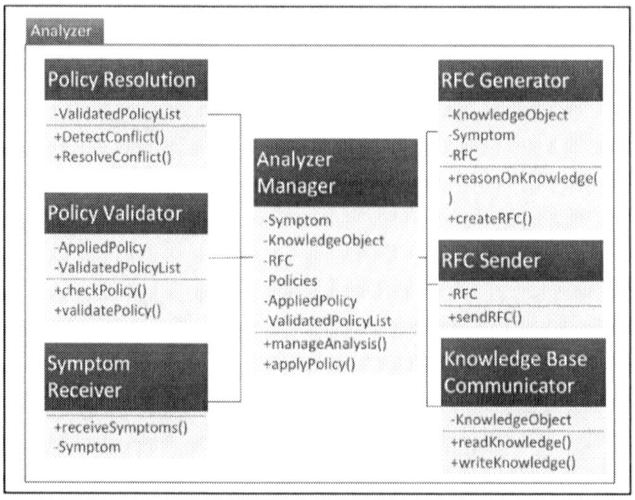

Figure 2. Frameself Analyzing Model.

E. Planning

When the RfC is received, it will be transformed in a policy and interpreted be able to plan the change in the operational system using the KB (Figure 3). When this has been done, the plan will be sent to the Execution process. The Planner Manager method is taking care of the coordination, while the KBC shares the *effectors* and policies to apply.

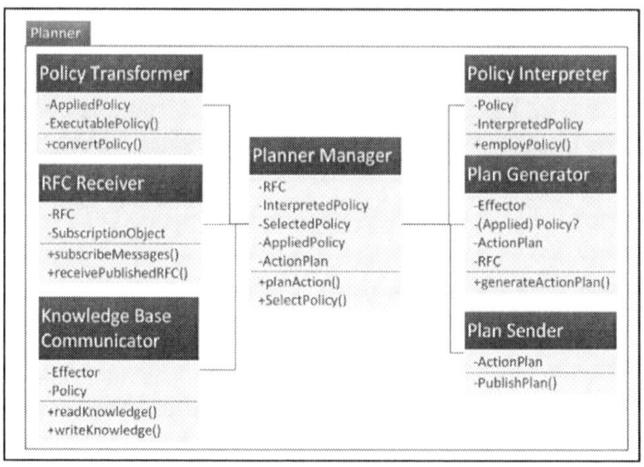

Figure 3. Frameself Planning Model.

F. Execution

After the planning activities have created and a plan is shared to change the operational system, the Execution process will translate the plan into specific actions (interpreted). These actions are embedded in a workflow and the process execution is triggered by the Workflow Engine, scheduled, and dispatched for execution. A process orchestrator method takes care of the monitoring according to the plan. Again, the Executor manager method will take care of a smooth process and the KBC is used for knowledge exchange. The Execution elements are shown in Figure 4.

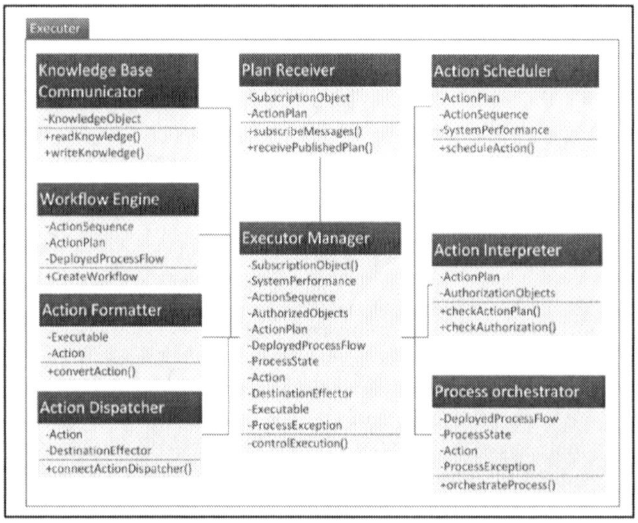

Figure 4. Frameself Execution Model.

G. Knowledge Base

In the KB, entities are created, changed read, and deleted. For each entity, a method is available, to do the job The Frameself architecture does not explicitly define how these methods are used. Also, the dynamics between the MAPE processes and the KB is related to each unique agent (Figure 5). Group learning or exchange of knowledge is not explicitly specified. This area of agent-interconnectedness needs to be studied in more detail.

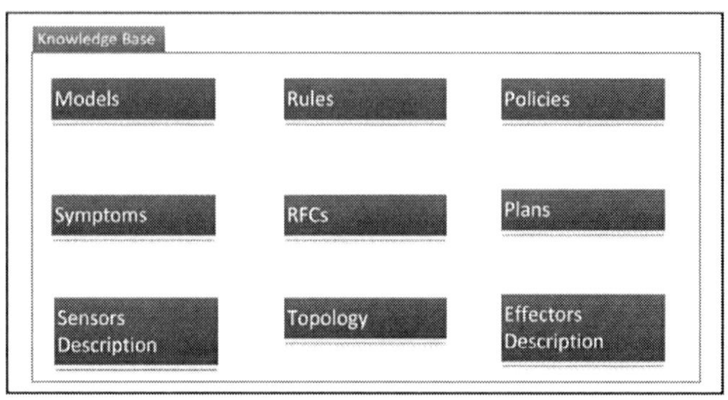

Figure 5. Frameself Knowledge Base Model.

When autonomic systems use the extended MAPE-K architecture to decide in runtime, a detailed understanding is required about what, where, when, how, and with what tools data are collected from the environment. Hence, the way the data are dimensioned, classified, and translated should be clarified before a proper analysis can be done. And when these data are analyzed, a suitable benchmark or expectation should be available to evaluate the performance of the system and applicability of business rules [41]. Based on this evaluation, the next operational process configuration is selected. But are the existing rules and processes appropriate for the state of the system in its context? This question requires the need for a meta-adaptation layer in which higher level evaluation, learning and verification is possible [42].

V. The Extended MAPE-K Model

In current research on the MAPE-K, attention for the influence of environmental factors is limited. More specifically, how does environmental factors like the participation of agents in a group influence the perception of environmental data and the evaluation principles of each single agent? Especially when the MAPE-K model is applied to distributed control loops with decentralized decision making, it could be interesting to see how the adaptation rules and results are shared amongst the other agents.

Recent initiatives aim at fine-tuning the MAPE-K model and dives into the characteristics of the KB. Research by Kloes *et al.* [42] show a MAPE-K extension, where the KB is described with four adaptation mechanisms: the Environment model K_{Env}, System model K_{Sys}, Goal model K_{Goal} and Adaptation model K_{Adapt}. Also, they added two components to enable meta-adaptation: Evaluation and Learning. Recently, they also added the Verification component to this [43]. With these extensions, the MAPE-K model logic becomes adaptive and applies dynamic, context specific rules. The first results from this study show that the adaptability of the process improves but should be validated to a higher extent to achieve generic applicability.

Within the Knowledge component, two mechanisms are subject to external factors: Knowledge of the Environment and Knowledge of Goal, while two other mechanisms are internal oriented: Knowledge of the System and Knowledge on the Adaptation actions. The Extended MAPE-K [43] shows how autonomous decision-making techniques in a runtime environment can be used to adapt to continuously changing environments in a quantitative manner. Guards monitor the environment and activate or de-activate specific system- or sub-goals. So, these guards are trained to make the system context sensitive. In the study of Kloes et al [43], a model for Goal requirements definition is proposed, where a parent goal can consist of sub-goals. These sub-goals could mutually reinforce and measured as weighted contributors to the parent-goal but can also be exclusive contributors. Together, the joint success rates of the set of sub-goals will determine the total success of the parent-goal and therefore the success of planned actions.

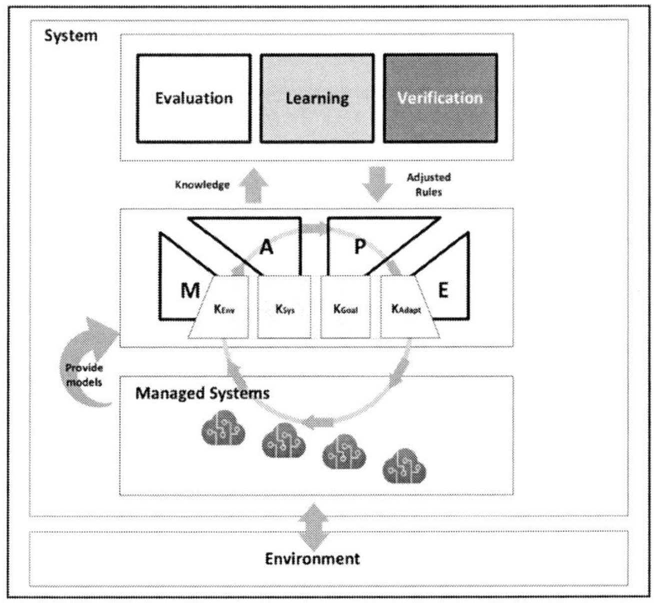

Figure 6. Extended MAPE-K model [43].

Taking notice of the agent driven decisions, how do we integrate the dominant logic of the group [62] in monitoring and adaptation activities in the extended MAPE-K control loop when applied to business processes? Previously, we saw that guards activate or de-activate goals, based on the state of the environment. But how are these guards positioned in the MAS model? Will they be event handlers or connectors that are triggered externally? And what about the data, which are stored in the Logical Operational Environment [45] and analyzed during decision making? These data are applied in the decision-making process, where the environmental-state, (sub)goals and guiding-principles come together [62]. What if the guiding-principles are influenced by the dominant logic of the group? Where do we store and maintain those principles? And how does an agent identify itself with a group, understand their rules of engagement and gain the required trust level? Or in other words, how could the environment be influenced to each actor's own advantage? A complex responsive process view on MAS control-cycles should take these considerations into account.

VI. Complex Responsive Processes of Relating

Organizations operate in a complex environment, which is characterized by emergence, nonlinearity, and self-organization [46][47]. In organization science, the organization, as the locus of attention, has been studied as a

Complex Adaptive System (CAS), where micro-dynamics of local interactions between the organizational actors result in global patterns [48][49]. Although this approach distinct the several steps of complexity [50], the single organizational actor is constituted as a rule-driven agent [51]. However, the full range of human experiences is hardly captured [52] while the environment is perceived as social and complex patterns, in which behavior of human actor is both physical and cognitive. Complex intelligence, where knowledge is created out of the social interaction, includes this human factor, but lacks a suitable integration with the idea of CAS [53]. This has been identified by Stacey et al as *Complex Responsive Processes of Relating* (CRP) [54], where activity of actors is influenced by the behavior of other actors, individuals, or groups. CRP, however, is taking both perspectives on human interaction and emergence in consideration [7].

According to Homan [55, p. 495] "the complex responsive process perspective does not assume the [agents] to be more or less mechanistic entities (automatons) reacting in a rule-driven fashion to their neighbors, but 'endows' the [agent] with thoughts, reflections, emotions, anxieties, ambitions, socialization, history, political games, spontaneity, unpredictability, and uncertainty, also understanding (human) interactions with others as intrinsic power relations." In the CRP setting, actors will search for others to create a critical mass or are complementary in capabilities or skills [56] to overcome uncertainty. These groups are formed around shared *themes*, which is shared, repetitive and enduring in its values, beliefs, traditions, habits, routines, and procedures [54].

From the Social Feedback Theory [57] we learned that the behavior of the agent is influenced by the group the agent belongs to. Agents perceive their environment through the lens of the group and act accordingly, based on its dominant logic [62]. Gergen describes this behavior as *social constructionism* [58]. According to Gergen, relationships in the group and the reality of group members are socially constructed and are limited by culture, history, and human embeddedness in the physical world. Not the individual mind but the relationship becomes the main driver for dynamics. The gesture and response dynamics in group activities are triggered by environmental artifacts and lead to the application and creation of patterns and the disclosure of new artifacts to the environment, which is, according to Stacey [59] the true source of knowledge creation. So, according to the CRP theory, to understand the dynamics of a system, one should focus on the interaction of actors in groups instead of individual behavior [54].

VII. CRP AS ACCELERATOR FOR A SELF-ADAPTING MULTI-AGENT SYSTEM

The effort to include CRP in a MAS system architecture will start with the meta model definition of a MAS. A pragmatic model for MAS architecture is the SARL metamodel [63], which describes the entities that construct the building blocks for a MAS system. Each agent will act in its context, composed of one or multiple spaces. Within this meta model, the interaction model is created, that is derived from the Physical and Social space. The interaction model will group together the several agents and describes the interaction patterns with use of relevant information flows. These information flows are based on the relevant dimensions (descriptions of artifacts) in its environment and influenced by the dominant group logic and semiotics in the system space. Environmental knowledge is perceived through guards and actions are taken to effectuate agent behavior in its environment. This will result in emergent interaction patterns within the Opportunity Space [44].

The adaptive process of a MAS is described by the (extended) MAPE-K model. Environmental events trigger the control cycle, resulting in the execution of the sub-system and a super-system learning cycle (Evaluation, Learning, Verification). Each step in the extended MAPE-K model is probably be influenced by the interaction with other agents and knowledge is shared [42]. The share of knowledge could catalyze the decision-making process in MAS platforms and could be a possible solution to reduce uncertainty in time critical, runtime environments. Also, it will stimulate the coherence of group actions and controllability of MAS behavior. But what elements in the KB are shared and how will this influence the behavior of the agent in the MAPE-K control cycle? Especially the effectiveness and timeliness of the agent's response is an interesting element in knowledge exchange.

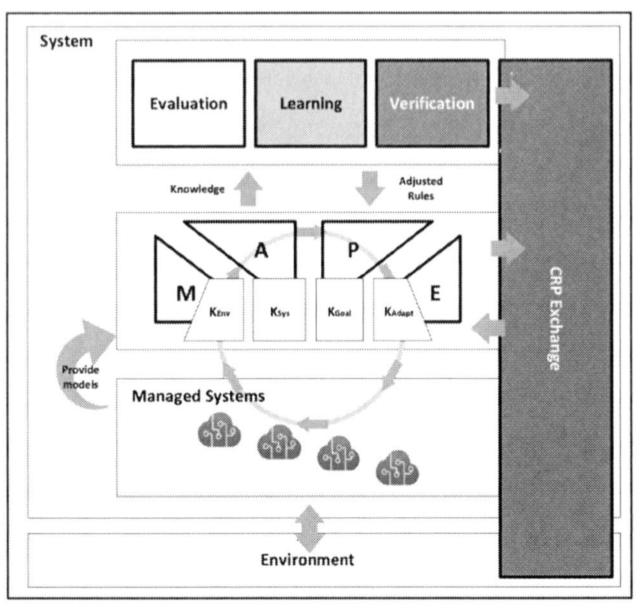

Figure 7. MAPE-K CRP model.

The solution will be a dialectics platform, where groups of agents apply gestures and respond to that. On this platform, a set of formal patterns is available to support these processes. Agents will raise questions and receive feedback from other agents. This will result in dialectics, where new entities are created that could be used in the agent's own knowledge base. Based on this concept, the research should investigate how the meta model and architecture should look like. Also it has to describe the formalize methods for information exchange. This extension can be labelled as the "MAPE-K CRP model", that includes the CRP Exchange of Gesture and Response between agents (Figure 7).

VIII. Conclusions and Further Work

In this position paper the control cycle for Multi-Agent Systems is described, including possible extensions. Current models lack the social dialectics between agents. The instance in which the gesture and response between agents takes place should be added to the model. Further research is required to include social elements of emergent behavior in a Multi-Agent setting. This could accelerate the exchange of knowledge and ability to adapt. The next steps will be the development of the CRP MAPE-K extension architecture and the translation into a meta model including formal methods for development.

References

[1] R. Govert, "From place marketing to place," Place Branding and Public Diplomacy, vol. 7, no. 4, p. 227 – 231, 2011.

[2] S. de Leeuw, A. R. van Goor, and P. van Amstel, "The selection of distribution control techniques," The Int. Journal of Logistics Man., vol. 10, no. 1, pp. 97-112, 1999.

[3] M. Baddeley, "Herding, social influence and economic decision-making: socio-psychological and neuroscientific analyses," Philosophical Transactions of the Royal B Society, no. 365, pp. 281-90, 2010.

[4] M. E. Porter, "How Competitive Forces Shape Strategy," Harvard Business Review, 1979.

[5] M. E. Porter and M. R. Kramer, "Creating Shared Value," Harvard Business Review, vol. 89, no. 2, pp. 62-77, 2011.

[6] L. Tesfatsion, "Agent-based Computational Economics: A Constructive Approach to Economic Theory," in Handbook of Computational Economics, vol. Volume 2, Amsterdam, North-Holland, 2008, pp. 831-882.

[7] R. Stacey and D. Griffin, A Complexity Perspective on Researching Organizations, London: Routledge, 2005.

[8] G. C. Harcourt and P. A. Riach, "The General Theory: Volume 2 Overview, Extensions, Method and New Developments," New York, Routledge, 1997, pp. 284-99.

[9] Q. Long, "A flow-based three-dimensional collaborative decision-making model for supply-chain networks," Knowledge-Based Systems, no. 97, pp. 101-110, 2016.

[10] M. Watson, S. Hoormann, P. Capioppi and J. Jayaraman, Supply Chain Network Design: Understanding the Optimization behind Supply Chain Design, Amazon Digital Services, 2012.

[11] B. R. Tukamuhabwa, M. Stevenson, J. Busby, and M. Zorzini, "Supply chain resilience: definition, review and theoretical foundations for further study," Int. Journal of Production Research, vol. 53, no. 18, pp. 5592-5623, 2015.

[12] L. Ferrara, M. Marcellino, and M. Mogliani, "Macroeconomic forecasting during the Great Recession: The The return of non-linearity?," Int. Journal of Forecasting, vol. 31, no. 3, pp. 264-279, 2015.

[13] N. Driessen, B. P. H. Hillebrand, and S. Smolner, "Market innovation: A literature review and new research directions," Journal of Business Research, no. 123, pp. 450-462, 2021.

[14] M. Giannakis and M. Louis, "A Multi-AgentBased System with Big-Data Processing for Enhanced Supply Chain Agility," Journal of Enterprise Information Man., vol. 29, no. 5, pp. 1-19, 2016.

[15] R. Agarwal, R. Echambadi, A. M. Franco, and M. B. Sarkar, "Knowledge Transfer through Inheritance: Spin-out Generation, Development, and Survival," Academy of Man. Journal, no. 47, pp. 501-22, 2004.

[16] T. L. Friedman, The World is Flat, Canada: Douglas & McIntyre Ltd., 2005.

[17] H. K. Steensma and M. A. Lyles, "Explaining IJV Survival in a Transitional Econ-omy through Social Exchange and Knowledge-Based Perspectives," Strategic Man. Journal, vol. 21, no. 8, pp. 831-51, 2000.

[18] B. S. Fugate, J. T. Mentzer, D. J. Flint, "The role of logistics in market orientation," Journal of Business Logistics, vol. 29, no. 2, pp. 1-26, 2008.

[19] L. Boddedy and C. Ram, Execution: The Discipline of Getting Things Done, New York: Crown Business, 2002.

[20] E. M. Olson, S. F. Slater, G. Hult, and M. Thomas, "The Performance Implications of Fit among Business Strategy, Marketing Organization Structure, and Strategic Behavior," Journal of Marketing, vol. 69, no. 3, pp. 49-65, 2005.

[21] S. A. Zahra and G. George, "Absorptive Capacity: A Review, Reconceptualization, and Extension," Academy of Man. review, vol. 27, no. 2, pp. 185-203, 2002.

[22] T. Bui, "Building agent-based corporate information systems: An applicationto telemedicine," European Journal of Operational Research, vol. 122, no. 2, pp. 242-57, 2000.

[23] A-P. Hameria and A. Paatelab, "Supply networkdynamics as a source of new business," Int. Journal of Production Economics, no. 98, pp. 41-55, 2005.

[24] D. Pereira, E. Oliveirat, N. Moreira, and L. Sarmentot, "Towards an Architecture for Emotional BDI Agents," in IEEE Portuguese conference on artificial intelligence, Covilha, PT, 2005.

[25] Banisch, Sven; Gaisbauer, Felix; Olbrich, Eckehard, "How social feedback processing in the brain shapes collective opinion processes," ODYCCEUS - Opinion Dynamics and Cultural Conflict in European Spaces, Leipzig, 2020.

[26] H. Leibenstein, "Bandwagon, Snob, and Veblen Effects in the Theory of Consumers' Demand," The Quarterly Journal of Economics, vol. 64, no. 2, pp. 183-207, 1950.

[27] X. Xue, J. Dou, and Y. Shang, "Blockchain-driven supply chain decentralized operations – information sharing perspective," Business Process Man. Journal, vol. 27, no. 1, pp. 184-203, 2021.

[28] A. Dolgui, D. Ivanov, B. V. Sokolov, "Reconfigurable supply chain: the X-network," Int. Journal of Prod. Research, vol. 68, no. 13, pp. 4138-4163, 2020.

[29] C. Krupitzer, M. Breitbach, F. M. Roth, S. VanSyckel, G. Schiele, and C. Becker, "A Survey on Engineering Approaches for Self-Adaptive Systems. (Extended Version)," Pervasive and Mobile Computing, vol. 17, Part B, pp. 184-206, 2015 / revised in 2018.

[30] T. de Wolf andT. Holvoet, "Towards Autonomic Computing: Agent-Based Modelling, Dynamical Systems Analysis, and Decentralised Control," in Proc. INDIN, IEEE,, 2003.

[31] D. Fisch, M. Janicke, E. Kalkowski, and B. Sick, "Techniques for Knowledge Acquisition in Dynamically," Transactions on Autonomous and Adaptive Systems, vol. 7, no. 1, pp. 1-25, 2012.

[32] R. C. Cardoso and A. Ferrando, "A Review of Agent-Based Programming for Multi-Agent Systems," Computers, vol. 10, no. 16, pp. 1-15, 2021.

[33] J. Y. C. Chen, S. G. Lakhmani, K. Stowers, A. R. Selkowitz, J. L. Wright, and M. Barnes, "Situation Awareness-Based Agent Transparency and Human-Autonomy Teaming Effectiveness," Theoretical Issues in Ergonomics Science, vol. 19, no. 3, pp. 259–282, 2018.

[34] S. Daronnat, L. Azzopardi, M. Halvey, and M. Dubiel, "Inferring Trust From Users' Behaviours; Agents' Predictability Positively Affects Trust, Task Performance and Cognitive Load in Human-Agent Real-Time Collaboration," Frontiers in Robotics and AI, vol. 8, pp. 1-14, 2021.

[35] M. J. Wooldridge, The Logical Modelling of Computational Multi-Agent Systems, Manchester: University of Manchester, Institute of Science and Technology, Department of Computation, 1992.

[36] Y-Y. Liu and A-L. Barabasi, "Control principles of complex systems," REVIEWS OF MODERN PHYSICS, vol. 88, no. July-September, pp. 1-58, 2016.

[37] J. O. Kephart, and D. M. Chess, "The vision of autonomic computing," IEEE Computer Society, pp. 41-50, 2003.

[38] P. Arcaini, E. Riccobene, and P. Scandurra, "Formal Design and Verification of Self-Adaptive Systems with Decentralized Control," ACM Transactions on Autonomous and Adaptive Systems,, vol. 2017, no. 4, pp. 1-35, 2017.

[39] D. Weyns, B. Schmerl, V. Grassi, S. Malek, R. Mirandola, C. Prehover, J. Wuttke, J. Andersson, H. Giese, and K. M. Göschka, "Dagstuhl Seminar on Software Engineering," in On Patterns for Decentralized Control in Self-Adaptive Systems, October 2010.

[40] M. B. Alaya and T. Monteil, "FRAMESELF: A generic autonomic framework for self-management of distributed systems - Application on the self-configuration of M2M architecture using semantic and ontology," in Int. Conference on Collaboration Technologies and Infrastructures, Toulouse (F), 2012.

[41] V. Kloes, T. Goethel, and S. Glesner, "Runtime management and quantitative evaluation of changing system goals in complex autonomous systems," The Journal of Systems & Software, no. 144, pp. 314-327, 2018.

[42] V. Kloes, T. Goethel, and S. Glesner, "Adaptive Knowledge Bases in Self-Adaptive System Design," in 41st Euromicro Conference on Software Engineering and Advanced Applications, 2015.

[43] V. Kloes, T. Goethel, and S. Glesner, "Comprehensible and dependable self-learning self-adaptive systems," Journal of Systems Architecture, no. 85-86, pp. 28-42, 2018.

[44] M. Schindehutte and M. H. Morris, "Advancing Strategic Entrepreneurship Research: The Role of Complexity Science in Shifting the Paradigm," Entrepreneurship Theory and Practice, pp. 241-276, 2009.

[45] J. Oukharijane, I. B. Said, M. A. Chaabane, E. Andonoff, and R. Bouaziz, "Towards a New Adaptation Engine for Self-Adaptation of BPMN Processes Instances," in Proc. of the 14th Int. Conference On Evaluation of Novel Approaches to Software Engineering (ENASE), Heraklion, GREECE, 2019.

[46] P. Anderson, "Complexity theory and organization science," Organization Science, vol. 10, no. 3, pp. 216-32, 1999.

[47] B. Burnes, "Complexity theories and organizational change," Int. Journal of Man. Review, vol. 7, no. 2, pp. 73-90, 2005.

[48] J. Goldstein, J. K. Hazy, and B. B. Lichtenstein, Complexity theories and organizational change, New York: PalGrave McMillan, 2010.

[49] J. K. Hazy, J. Goldstein, and B. B. Lichtenstein, Complexity and the Nexus of Leadership, Mansfield, MA: ISCE Publishing, 2007.

[50] P. A. Allen, M. Strathern, and J. S. Baldwin, "Evolutionary drive: New understanding of change in socio-economic systems," Complexity and the Nexus of Leadership, vol. 8, no. 2, pp. 2-19, 2006.

[51] R. Macintosh and D. MacLean, "Conditioned emergence: researching change and changing research," Int. Journal of Op. & Prod. Man., vol. 21, no. 10, pp. 1343-1357, 2001.

[52] S. Johansson and T. M. B. Aasen, "Exploring innovation processes from a complexity perspective. Part I: theoretical and methodological approach," Int. Journal of Learning and Change, vol. 2, no. 4, pp. 420-33, 2007.

[53] J. Inglis and M. Steele, "Complexity Intelligence and Cultural Coaching: Navigating the Gap Between Our Societal Challenges and Our Capacities," Integral Review, vol. 1, pp. 35-46, 2005.

[54] R. Stacey, Complexity and group processes: A radically social understanding of individuals, New York: Routledge, 2003,

[55] T. H. Homan, "Locating complex responsive process research in the approaches of theorising about organizations," Int. Journal of Business and Globalisation, vol. 17, no. 4, pp. 491-513, 2016.

[56] D. Stanley, "Complex Responsive Processes: An Alternative Interpretation of Knowledge, Knowing, and Understanding," Complicity: An Int. Journal of Complexity and Education, vol. 6, no. 1, p. 29 - 39, 2009.

[57] S. Banisch, F. Gaisbauer, and E. Olbrich, "How social feedback processing in the brain shapes collective opinion processes in the ear of social media," ArXiv -08154, 2013.

[58] K. J. Gergen, An Invitation to Social Construction, Thousand Oaks, CA: Sage, 1999.

[59] R. Stacey, Complex Responsive Processes in Organizations: Learning and Knowledge Creation, New York: Routledge, 2001.

[60] F. Golpayegani, I. Dusparic, and S. Clark, "Using Social Dependence to Enable Neighbourly Behaviour in Open Multi-Agent Systems." ACM Transactions on Intelligent Systems and Technology, vol. 10, no.3, pp 1-31, 2019.

[61] P. Arcaini, E. Riccobene, and P. Scandurra, "Modelling and Analyzing MAPE-K Feedback Loops for Self-Adaptation.", 10th Int. Symposium on Software Engineering for Adaptive and Self-Managing Systems, 2015.

[62] T, Bose, A. Reina, and J. A. R. Marshall, "Collective Decision-Making," Current Opinion in Behavioral Sciences, no. 16, pp 30-34, 2017.

[63] S. Galland, S. Rodriguez, and N. Gaud, "Run-time environment for the SARL agent-programming language: the example of the Janus platform," in Future Generation Computer Systems, 2017.

Negligible Details - Towards Abstracting Source Code to Distill the Essence of Concepts

Christian Schindler*, Mirco Schindler† and Andreas Rausch‡
Institute for Software and Systems Engineering
Clausthal University of Technology
Clausthal, Germany
* Email: christian.schindler@tu-clausthal.de
† Email: mirco.schindler@tu-clausthal.de
‡ Email: andreas.rausch@tu-clausthal.de

***Abstract*—Design and architecture patterns are proven domain-independent solution approaches for common problems occurring in the development of software systems. To guarantee the problem-solving capabilities of patterns, a correct implementation of the design pattern is essential. As a context-specific adoption of the design pattern to the software system needs to be performed by the developers, we argue that their comprehension plays a crucial role in the creation and maintenance of such correct implementations over the system's lifespan. Even with migration and integration of legacy components into an adaptive System, where other paradigms are used, for example, must be compatible on a conceptual level. The primary intent of this paper is to separate essential syntactic information from varying aspects, given a set of implementation samples. We introduce an approach that abstracts given object-oriented implementations by semantically resolving and splitting an Abstract Syntax Tree into small paths. In analyzing paths from given samples we build a shared concept. In this paper, we build the shared concept from 230 example implementations containing the singleton design pattern and 230 counterexamples to classify new unseen java classes. The contribution this paper provides is composed of three parts. (i) A novel approach to abstract object-oriented code, (ii) an interpretable way to identify common parts extracted from multiple abstractions, and (iii) a way to classify unseen samples to implement the same concept.**

***Index Terms*—Software Abstraction, Object Oriented Language, Design Pattern, Source Code Comprehension, Software Architecture**

I. INTRODUCTION

Design patterns have been established for reusing proven solutions to a class of problems. Nevertheless, especially for a dynamic adaptive system, the correct implementation of adaptation mechanisms is essential for the quality of the overall system. Patterns are described informally or semi-formally as context-independent solution concepts. As a consequence, in order to apply a design pattern, it is necessary to embed it into the actual implementation context; to do so, a common understanding of the concept provided by the pattern had to be established [1], [2].

To relate implementation and architecture, the Unified Modeling Language (UML), for example, offers the mechanism of collaborations within the context of a composition structure diagram and the context-specific embedding in a given domain. Here, the description is separated from the actual application in modeling. Collaborations describe the composition of roles, which must be linked to specific parts of the application [3], [4].

Faulty implementations of patterns may produce functionally correct solutions but may lack the (mainly) non-functional properties provided by the pattern, such as specific modularity goals or specifications from the software architecture [5]. Inaccurate implementations can emerge not only in the initial implementation of the pattern but also from side effects introduced with changes, even elsewhere in the codebase [6], [7]. In particular, in a scenario where system parts and components are implemented and maintained heterogeneously and by different companies and development teams, as is unavoidable in an adaptive Software Ecosystem, for example [8].

If a legacy system or component is to be migrated and integrated, for example, to satisfy a specific adaptation mechanism, it is necessary to check the current implementation's compatibility. For this, it is helpful to find design patterns in existing code to comprehend the whole system better. Especially if it is written by other developers or not further documented. With a focus on code comprehension, it is necessary to extract more complex architectural patterns from simple code patterns iteratively. As a starting point, this paper contributes to recognizing design patterns by generating a data-driven interpretable representation of the design pattern from a set of implementation examples and counterexamples. No formal specification of the design pattern beforehand is needed.

This paper addresses the following **Research Questions (RQs)**: RQ1: Is it possible to abstract different concrete implementations of the same architectural design pattern so that the abstractions show a similarity? RQ2: Is it possible to formulate what the shared concept consists of across multiple samples? RQ3: Is it possible to classify unseen samples using the introduced formulation mechanism?

Section 2 gives foundations on programming languages and the construction of the Abstract Syntax Trees (ASTs). Section 3 introduces the source code abstraction approach alongside two different levels of abstraction. Section 4 is the evaluation of the stated RQs with a discussion of the results and limitations. Section 5 presents an overview of related work. Finally, the conclusion and an outline of future work are given in Section 6.

II. FOUNDATION

This paper investigates the compositionality of abstract concepts. The inputs for the presented approach are syntactically correct but not executable source code artifacts. The focus is, therefore, on the static structure of a program. This structure is defined by the syntactic and semantic rules of a programming language. Each programming language consists of a set of programming concepts and specified paradigms, applying to modern programming languages that do not strictly follow one paradigm [9].

These concepts, defined by the programming language, are called **atomic concepts** in the following and manifest themselves in the source code by the language's **keywords**. Programming languages are formal languages because they consist of words over a given and finite alphabet [10]. Thus, the words are well-formed concerning a fixed and finite set of formal production rules [11]. Moreover, the lexical grammar of a programming language is usually context-free [12].

A grammar G consists of a four-tuple.

$$G(N, \Sigma, R, S) \tag{1}$$

with N : finite set of nonterminal symbols,
disjoint with the strings produced from G.
Σ : finite set of terminal symbols, disjoint from N.
R : finite set of production rules: $N \rightarrow (\Sigma \cup N)^*$
where * is the kleene star operator.
S : distinguished start symbol, $S \in N$.

We focus on object-oriented programming languages. Consequently, the type-system plays an important role and can be understood as an assurance to operations and documentation that can not be outdated. Types predefined by the programming language are so-called **atomic types**. Out of these atomic types, abstract types are constructed. The step of abstraction, which is also the foundation of the principle of information hiding, of abstract types is the structure defined by fields and an interface specified by the operations.

Since the languages considered here are formal, an automaton can be specified, which can process the character stream of the source code artifact. This is also the first step in compiling a program. Figure 1 shows the steps relevant to this paper of analyzing a program by a compiler. First, a scanner transforms the input stream into a language-specific token stream during lexical analysis. The tokens are also significant parts of a program, as they contain the atomic concepts of the programming language. This step reduces complexity, aggregates character, and identifies keywords. Then, a tree is generated from the token stream during syntactic analysis. A **tree** is a recursive data structure and a particular type of graph structure (a formal definition can be found in III-D) with a dedicated root node and containing no cycles. Finally, each recognized token is converted to a node in the tree. Than, a semantic analysis is performed since not all rules, especially context-dependent ones, can be checked during derivation. This step also resolves the types, names and annotates the tree's nodes to reflect this. Therefore, a symbol table is used to map each symbol with associated information like type and scope.

Through the instantiation of types, another kind of context-dependencies arises, which leads to the fact that the semantic meaning of a word derived by the grammar is no longer unique.

The challenge in extracting higher-level concepts up to architectural concepts is that these concepts are not included as concepts in the programming language. Instead, these can be understood as the composition of atomic concepts within a respective context. For program comprehension, it is essential to get a precise understanding of the concepts used in the implementation. Therefore with the increasing complexity and evolution of the program describing the essence of a concept in a comprehensible way to humans is a critical task.

It follows directly from the chosen class of language type that the set of generated concepts is countably infinite. Also, the set of reference implementations is infinite, with the difficulty that the same concept can be implemented in different ways. Thus, similarity could not be detected with a simple comparison of source code snippets.

III. SOURCE CODE REPRESENTATION

The main objective is a way to represent object-oriented source code samples on an abstract level compared to the raw source code files to enable interpretability on common parts and differences. Reducing information such as the naming of elements (e.g., methods, variables) or the order in which parts of the snippet (methods, variables) are declared or logic is handled (e.g., cases in a switch statement) help in this approach as it distracts from syntactical similarities.

We introduce two different levels of abstraction that both allow the expression of smaller parts reoccurring across different valid code snippets following the language's grammar rules. The **abstraction level** $High$ (section III-B) is more abstract than level Low (section III-C). The more concrete level of abstraction has superior expressiveness as it adds constraints across multiple reoccurring parts and allows for the distinction of elements (e.g., methods, variables).

We will elaborate on our general approach (section III-A), being identical for both levels of abstraction first, then elaborating on $High$(section III-B), and adding in how we use the concept of uniquely identifying parts in Low. In section III-C we explain how such constraints are added. In section III-D we address how abstractions of different samples can be compared. Section III-E introduces the shared concept and how to construct it based on given code samples.

A. Source code abstraction approach

The approach, as illustrated in Figure 2, takes source code of arbitrary size as an input to generate an abstract representation

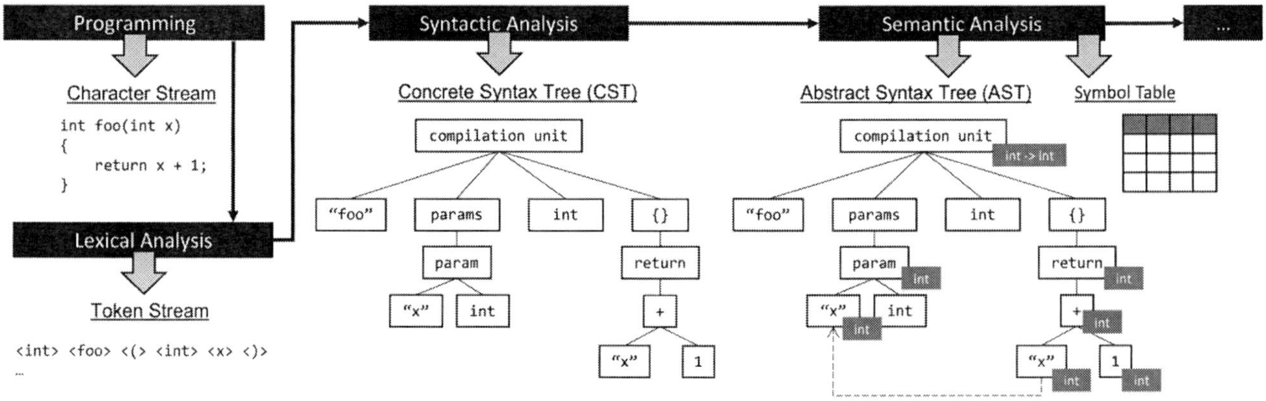

Fig. 1: First steps of a compilation process [12]

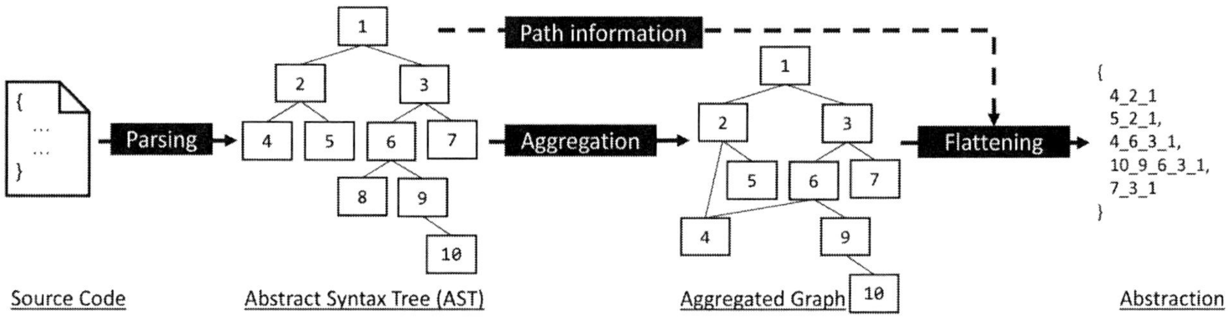

Fig. 2: Overall approach of the source code abstraction

in the form of a set of *Strings* that represent its syntax with additional information from the semantic analysis and aggregation. The Strings are sequences of tokens retrieved while processing the input that does not need to be exact sequences of the *Lexical Analysis*, as shown in Figure 1. A detailed walk through example can be found in sections III-B and III-C, Figure 1 contains only an illustrative one.

We analyse the code snippets *AST* to get a syntactic representation of the sample. The AST tokens get resolved during the aggregation phase constructing an *Aggregated Graph*. By combining the *ASTs* paths and the *Aggregated Graph*, we create the flattened *Abstraction*.

Subsequently, we formalize the required representations (AST, Graph, and the Abstraction) and concepts (path, aggregation function). Based on these definitions, we introduce the idea of a shared concept.

We define the **graph** $g \in$ GRAPH by the following signature:

$$g(V,E) := \{V = \{v_1, v_2, \ldots, v_n\}, E \subseteq V \times V\} \quad (2)$$

with V : finite indexed set of nodes.
E : finite indexed and ordered set of directed edges $\{v_i, v_j\}$

and a **tree** $t \in$ GRAPH being a special cycle-free graph with a root node v_{root} and a set of leaf nodes V_{leaf}

$$t(V, E, v_{root}, V_{\text{leaf}}) := \{g(V,E), v_{root}, V_{\text{leaf}}\} \quad (3)$$

$$\begin{aligned} \text{with } & V_{\text{leaf}} \subset V \wedge v_{\text{root}} \in V \\ & \forall v \in V \nexists v \mid \{v_{\text{root}}, v\} \in E \\ & \forall v_{\text{leaf}} \in V_{\text{leaf}} \nexists v \mid \{v, v_{leaf}\} \in E \end{aligned}$$

A path p in a tree t is a sequence of nodes V connected by edges E. The first node needs to be a leaf node and the final node needs to be the root node v_{root} of t.

$$p(V,E) := \{V,E\} \quad (4)$$

$$\begin{aligned} \text{with } & V := \{v_i \mid 1 \leq i \leq n\} \\ & v_1 \in t(V_{leaf}) \wedge v_n = t(v_{root}) \\ & E := \{\{v_{j-1}, v_j\} \mid 2 \leq j \leq n\} \end{aligned}$$

In the *Aggregation* step, the nodes of the AST get mapped to nodes of a resulting *Aggregated Graph*, by an aggregation function $f_{\text{aggregate}}(t) := V_t \to V_g$.

To construct the abstract representation a a concrete aggregation function combines the information of all paths P of the

```
1 public class FooBar {
2         public void foo() {...}
3         public void bar() {...}
4 }
```

Fig. 3: Java implementation of a class with two methods - *program 1*

tree and the graph g itself. P is the set of paths containing each path from every leaf node of V_{leaf} to the root node v_{root}. It is defined by the following signature:

$$P := \{p \mid p(v_1) \in t(V_{\text{leaf}}) \wedge p(v_n) = t(v_{\text{root}}) \wedge \forall v_{\text{leaf}} \in t(V_{\text{leaf}}) \exists! p \mid v_{\text{leaf}} \in p(V)\} \quad (5)$$

An **abstraction** is defined by the function f_{abstract} :

$$f_{\text{abstract}}(t, f_{\text{aggregate}}(t)) := (V_t, E_t) \times (V_g, E_g) \rightarrow P \quad (6)$$

To obtain the flattened abstraction, we combine the path information from the tree and the node information from the aggregated graph. The structure of the flattened Strings in the abstraction comes from the Paths P in the AST. The information of the relevant nodes results from applying the $f_{\text{aggregate}}$ function to the nodes of the paths $p \in P$. The final abstraction is a set of all distinct flattened Strings. In the example Figure 2, the aggregation merges the nodes *4* and *8* (from the AST). Those nodes represent the same semantic unit (e.g., the same literal) In this case p is *"8_6_3_1"*, after applying $f_{\text{aggregate}}$ the flattened String is *"4_6_3_1"*.

B. Abstraction level *High*

The nodes (tokens) in an AST have additional traits. We utilize the type of the node, which indicates what part of the language the node reflects (e.g., the declaration of a class or the call of a method). In addition, we use the information of more basic nodes (e.g., keywords, primitive operators) to represent individual nodes per manifestation (e.g., *TRUE* and *FALSE* for *Boolean* values) and one node per *Modifier* (e.g., *PRIVATE, PUBLIC, and STATIC*). On *High*, the aggregation step summarizes all nodes of the same type (e.g., all nodes that declare methods) into a single node.

Figure 3 shows a short code snippet that we will use for both abstraction levels to illustrate the approach and the resulting representations. The sample consists of a *public class FooBar* containing two methods (*foo* and *bar*). The content of the methods is left out, as it would be hard to display the resulting ASTs and graphs. As illustrated in Figure 2, we start with traversing the AST. The resulting tree is shown in Figure 4. In the tree, we can see the individual statements reflected by nodes and corresponding edges. Each node contains the information of the type of the node (e.g., *ClassDeclaration* for the root element) and, if available additional information such as the reflecting values associated with the nodes (e.g., *SimpleNames* reflecting the name of the class *FooBar* and the names of the methods *foo* and *bar*) or the proper modifier (in this case *PUBLIC* in all instances).

The higher-level **aggregation rules** of nodes are: (i) resolve keywords from the language. This includes *Primitive Operators, Primitive Types, Modifiers, TRUE, FALSE*, and (ii) reduce other nodes to the assigned types.

Figure 6a shows the resulting graph by applying the aggregation rules. Our abstraction aims to (i) consist of multiple small parts (ii) likely to be contained in multiple samples. From the tree (Figure 4), the graph (Figure 6a), and the aggregation rules , it is possible to construct the paths in Figure 5. Here underscore separates the nodes in a flattened path.

Carried information *High*: The paths extracted carry certain information enabling reasoning about the original program. For example, the second path states that there is a *PUBLIC ClassDeclaration* (line 1 of the code sample in Figure 3). The third path states a *PUBLIC MethodDeclaration* in a *ClassDeclaration*. From the information contained in the abstraction, we cannot tell which methods *foo* or *bar* this particular path represents.

On *High*, we cannot conclude across multiple paths. For example, it is impossible to state that the *MethodDeclaration* from paths 3 and 4 are part of the same *Method*. On the one hand, this shows that the abstraction level is capable of reflecting general structures of the original code while being able to ignore the order of appearance in the original implementation. On the other hand, the abstraction lacks the distinction of different elements and the ability to connect multiple paths related to each other.

C. Abstraction level *Low*

The stated drawbacks of *High* get addressed at *Low*, containing more information from the original sample. The overall approach (Figure 2) still holds, with different steps in the aggregation phase. Semantic analysis of the AST is utilized to resolve elements. We introduce indices to those resolved elements, allowing the distinction of multiple nodes (of the same type and even across multiple types). The **aggregation rules** are as follows: (i) exactly as the first rule on *High*; (ii) identification of *Classes* and *Methods* by their signature; and (iii) resolution *(Simple)Names* with an index per unique name.

According to the stated rules, aggregation of the AST leads to the graph illustrated in Figure 6b. The indices allow the identification of elements. For example, we can still refer to the methods using index 1 and 2. The index is attached in the flat representation of the paths, separated by a hash symbol. The resulting paths of the code sample on *Low* are given in Figure 7. All the information of *High* is still contained in this representation, as it is possible to remove all the indices and remove the duplicated paths resulting in Figure 5.

Carried information *Low*: The indices allow (i) to conclude across multiple paths, (ii) to distinguish multiple elements of the same type (e.g., the two *Methods*), and (iii) to express constraints that join different types seen in the aggregation process to superior entities (e.g., using one index for a specific *MethodDeclaration* and *MethodCallExpression*).

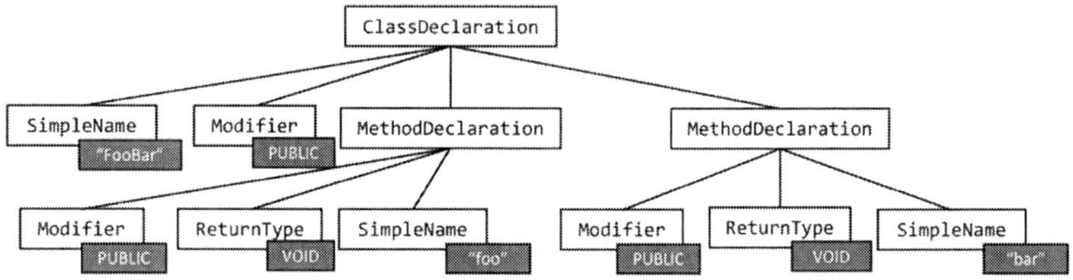

Fig. 4: AST of program 1

1 SimpleName_ClassDeclaration
2 PUBLIC_ClassDeclaration
3 PUBLIC_MethodDeclaration_ClassDeclaration
4 VOID_MethodDeclaration_ClassDeclaration
5 SimpleName_MethodDeclaration_ClassDeclaration

Fig. 5: Abstraction $High$ of program 1

In Figure 7, all the paths are in the context of to the same *ClassDeclaration(#1)*. We can draw conclusions about *MethodDeclaration(#1)* from paths 3 and 4 and state that it is *PUBLIC* and has the return type (*VOID*). The same holds for paths (6 and 7 respectively for the second *MethodDeclaration*). To distinguish elements across multiple paths the indices can be used similarly. We can tell that paths 5 and 6 are not belonging to the same *MethodDeclaration*.

D. Abstraction alignment

In the sections above, we introduced abstraction levels $High$ and Low for one single code snippet, both providing a set of paths representing the snippet. We showed how to reason across multiple paths of one abstraction. The next step in making use of the representation is to reason across multiple abstractions of different snippets x and y, by considering the sets of paths P_x and P_y, respectively, that they generate. We propose a *Jaccard Similarity* (Formula 7) based measurement, leading to a high similarity if a lot of paths are in both sets P_x and P_y, and little paths only in either set P_x or P_y.

$$jaccardSim(P_x, P_y) := \frac{\mid P_x \cap P_y \mid}{\mid P_x \cup P_y \mid} \tag{7}$$

On $High$ it is easy to be calculated without further steps needed, as no instance (e.g., multiple methods) are distinguished. On Low, the calculated similarity will depend on the indices assigned to the individual parts in the aggregation step, as the following example in Table I illustrates. The table is two-parts, with the upper part containing different paths (left-hand side) and three abstractions (P_a, P_{b1}, and P_{b2}). An x in the respective cell means that the path is part of the abstraction. The lower part of the table contains the pairwise Jaccard similarity. The similarity calculated differs between *jaccardSim*(P_a, P_{b1}) and *jaccardSim*(P_a, P_{b2}) regardless of both P_{b1} and P_{b2} being equally valid representations of a *Class* having one *PRIVATE* and one *PUBLIC Method*.

In the presented approach (Figure 2) the indices get assigned in order of node processing. If a node (e.g., a *MethodDeclaration*) has been seen before, the assigned index is reused, otherwise, the next available index (per node type) gets assigned. This could lead to P_{b1} or P_{b2} for the same code sample, that are equally valid abstractions.

The idea to counteract this is by aligning the samples to improve the similarity measured without alternating the information contained in the abstractions. We achieve this by looking for (sub)graph isomorphism and corresponding permutations. In this example, a similarity-maximizing permutation of P_{b2} regarding P_a would be to swap the indices of the two *MethodDeclarations*. An important remark is that such a swap of indices needs to conform to the **permutation rules** (i) the swap of indices needs to be done for all occurrences to not invalidate a constraint and (ii) entities need to be respected, so the index of such related types need to be aligned uniformly.

The **isomorphism** between two graphs is a *bijection* (one-to-one correspondence) between the nodes of the given graphs. As the graphs in our case are not guaranteed to be of the same size, we need to look into subgraph isomorphisms of the size of the smaller graph. A **subgraph** m of a graph g is denoted by:

$$m \subset g \iff V_m \subset V_s \wedge E_m \subset E_s \tag{8}$$

Finding such a *bijection* (candidate) of a subgraph consists of two steps, (i) fixing a suitable subgraph and the (ii) one-to-one correspondence. The verification of such a candidate can be done with the Formula 9. The graphs q and m are converted to adjacency matrices (see Formula 10) and the *bijection* is formulated as a **permutation matrix** Q. Q is constructed with the nodes of one graph as rows, and nodes of the other graph as columns, the cells representing a correspondence are filled with 1, all others with 0. An adjacency matrix D_m contains a row and column for each node of the graph m, the respective cell is filled with 1 if there is an edge between those nodes, with 0 otherwise.

Let q be a graph isomorphic to m, for some *permutation matrix* Q:

$$q \cong m \iff \exists Q, D_m = Q \times D_q \times Q^T \tag{9}$$

Let D_m be the **adjacency matrix** of m, with:

$$D_m ij := \begin{cases} 1 & \text{if } \{i, j\} \in E_m \\ 0 & \text{otherwise} \end{cases} \tag{10}$$

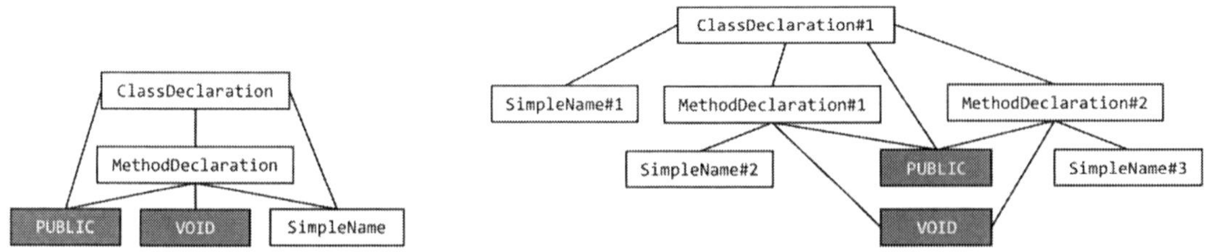

(a) Abstraction level *High* (b) Abstraction level *Low*

Fig. 6: Resulting graphs by aggregating nodes and edges of the example AST

TABLE I: SAMPLE ABSTRACTIONS AND CORRESPONDING PAIR-WISE JACCARD SIMILARITIES

paths on low abstraction level	P_a	P_{b1}	P_{b2}
PUBLIC_ClassDeclaration#1	x	x	x
PUBLIC_MethodDeclaration#1_ClassDeclaration#1	x	x	
VOID_MethodDeclaration#1_ClassDeclaration#1	x	x	x
PRIVATE_MethodDeclaration#1_ClassDeclaration#1			x
PUBLIC_MethodDeclaration#2_ClassDeclaration#1			x
VOID_MethodDeclaration#2_ClassDeclaration#1		x	x
PRIVATE_MethodDeclaration#2_ClassDeclaration#1		x	
jaccardSim with P_a	1	0.6	0.33
jaccardSim with P_{b1}	0.6	1	0.429
jaccardSim with P_{b2}	0.33	0.429	1

1 SimpleName#1_ClassDeclaration#1
2 PUBLIC_ClassDeclaration#1
3 PUBLIC_MethodDeclaration#1_ClassDeclaration#1
4 VOID_MethodDeclaration#1_ClassDeclaration#1
5 SimpleName#2_MethodDeclaration#1_ClassDeclaration#1
6 PUBLIC_MethodDeclaration#2_ClassDeclaration#1
7 VOID_MethodDeclaration#2_ClassDeclaration#1
8 SimpleName#3_MethodDeclaration#2_ClassDeclaration#1

Fig. 7: Abstraction *Low* of program 1

After an isomorphism has been found, the indices can be aligned according to the permutation, allowing for the final check to see if the resulting paths match. This is needed as g (and D_m) do not contain the information of the original paths, so the graph will accept possible paths not contained in the abstraction.

E. Shared concept

We define a shared concept c_{shared} as the set of similarities and differences between a set of code snippets. The abstractions of code snippets, which contain the concepts c_{shared} are elements of the set A_{in} and code snippets, which are not an implementation of the concept c_{shared} , represent an element of the set A_{ex}.

Out of these two sets of abstractions of examples and counterexamples, the representation of the shared concept is derived as follows:

$$c(A_{in}, A_{ex}) := \{P_{in}, P_{ex}\} \tag{11}$$

with $P_{in} \cap P_{ex} = \emptyset$

$$\forall p_{in} \in P_{in} \wedge \forall a_{in} \in A_{in} \mid p_{in} \in a_{in}$$
$$\forall p_{ex} \in P_{ex} \exists a_{ex} \in A_{ex} \mid p_{ex} \in a_{ex}$$
$$\forall p_{ex} \in P_{ex} \nexists a_{in} \in A_{in} \mid p_{ex} \in a_{in}$$

Related to the above definition, a shared concept is described by two sets of paths P_{in} and P_{ex}. Each path $p_{in} \in P_{in}$ is included in every single abstraction of A_{in}. P_{ex} consists of paths p_{ex} retrieved by the set of abstractions A_{ex}. For a path to be included in P_{ex} it needs to be in at least one abstraction of A_{ex} and must not be in any abstraction of A_{in}. The idea of those exclusion paths is to handle paths seen in the programming language that have never been seen in a positive example that is expected to include the shared concept. By including samples from different repositories and business domains into the sets A_{in} and A_{out} we hypothesize that the shared concept is containing business-domain-independent overlap.

IV. Evaluation

The evaluation starts with describing the data set, which was collected, and annotated by the authors. The second part introduces the singleton design pattern, as this is the case study through the evaluation of the paper. The rest of the section addresses the stated RQs. We start by finding similarities on the abstraction levels (RQ1) calculating pair-wise jaccard similarities on the abstraction levels and analyze how the similarity compares on pairs that are both singletons, one of the samples being a singleton and non of the samples being a singleton. We formulate the shared concept as RQ2, by including all paths P_{in} we have seen in all samples (of the

TABLE II: ANALYSIS OF THE AMOUNTS OF PATHS IN THE ABSTRACTIONS

	min # of paths		max # of paths		avg. # of paths	
	low	high	low	high	low	high
singleton	17	17	2379	646	247.26	88.61
non singleton	6	4	2856	983	421.16	157.37
all samples	6	4	2856	983	334.21	122.99

singleton), in addition, we formulated an exclusion set of paths P_{ex}, by specifically excluding paths that we have only seen in non-singleton samples.

Classifying new samples on the abstraction levels using the formulated shared concept (RQ3) is done as the last part of the evaluation.

A. Results

1) Preprocessing of the data set: The data set (*java-singleton*) collected and used to evaluate the abstraction approach consists of 230 java code samples labeled as part of this paper, containing the singleton design pattern and 230 additional samples that do not implement the singleton design pattern. The classes originate from different projects. The labels were applied by two authors, only containing samples that were confirmed by both authors. We chose the singleton pattern as a concept to evaluate as it combines a few criteria we consider beneficial as a showcase in this paper. The purpose of the pattern is widely understood and used in practice. The implementation is all in one place (the singleton class), leaving aside large search spaces [13]. Making it reasonable to identify samples in existing code, but leaving room for the implementation to vary. It introduces manageable complexity to the task at hand while enabling us to collect a data set to evaluate the presented work, although the presented approach of abstraction is not limited to the scope of a single class, file, or pattern. We abstracted all the samples on both levels of abstraction. Table II gives insights into the resulting abstractions. The table contains the minimum, maximum, and average amount of paths all abstractions of a given set of abstraction. The sets show that the range on how many paths are in the samples varies a lot for each given set inspected. The average is also significantly higher than the minimum amount of paths of a sample, indicating that on average there are things in the samples than they can share (as this is what at most can be overlap).

2) Results RQ1: As described in section III-D we are going to measure similarity using the *Jaccard Similarity* (Formula 7). Table III summarizes details on the calculated similarities. Each row represents ten percent incremental thresholds, with the corresponding amount of sample pairs that are at least as similar as the threshold requires. The reported numbers are broken down into how many pairs are (i) both singletons, (ii) one of them is a singleton and, (iii) none of them is a singleton. This is done for both abstraction levels. The comparison of the samples with itself is excluded from the table.

The data shown in the table support the assumption that the abstractions embody similarity related to the singleton design pattern. From the columns *both singleton* on both abstraction levels we take that the stated RQ1 holds and that it is possible to abstract different concrete implementations of the same design pattern to show a similarity. As the similarity observed is significantly higher compared to the other columns in the table.

3) Results RQ2: We built a shared concept as introduced in our Definition 11. This part of the evaluation is limited to $High$ as no complete alignment of all samples has been calculated, leading to inaccurate results on Low. More on this is addressed in the limitations and future work section of the paper.

We follow common practice in Natural Language Processing (NLP) (compare stop word removal [14]) and trim the data so that we do not rely on too (un)common paths. We only keep paths in at least 5 percent and at most 95 percent of the samples of the dataset.

Table IV distinguishes the (non-)trimmed abstractions. It displays the number of paths belonging to specific subsets of the data set. For the non-trimmed row, many paths are exclusive to (non-)singletons ($4644 + 12813$) compared to a 1996 part shared. As the collected data set is small, contributing to infrequently observed paths, we focus on the trimmed column of the table. There are no paths left that are exclusive to the singleton samples. Allows us to ascertain, that there are no language constructs exclusively used to implement the singletons. In addition, eight paths are exclusive to non-singleton samples, which indicates that they are part of the programming language but not used to implement the singleton design pattern. No paths are seen across all non-singleton samples. The majority of paths are seen across both singletons and non-singletons. The shared concept retrieved from the data set *java-singleton* consists of twelve paths in P_{in} and eight paths in P_{ex}.

4) Results RQ3: To evaluate if it is possible to use the shared concept for classification of unseen code, we use a dataset [15] providing annotations of used design patterns. The dataset contains annotations for the following nine java projects: *QuickUML 2001, Lexi, JRefactory, Netbeans, JUnit, MapperXML, Nutch, PMD, and JHotDraw.*

The authors of this paper validated the annotations. From the 13 annotations, we rejected seven, finding six additional singleton implementations that were not annotated as such before. Resulting in a total of 12 instances.

We conducted three experiments (Table. V)(i) *High incl.* only looking to include all the P_{in} paths, (ii) $High$ refers to in addition looking that none of the exclusion paths P_{ex} are present, and (iii) Low we used the inclusion paths P_{in} and associated indices that conform to the singleton pattern (described in Section 5.2.). Here we then aligned the indices of the samples (using subgraph isomorphism).

As a given sample can be classify containing a singleton (*Positive*) or not (Negative) and the ground truth label can tell if it is a singleton or not, we end up with the resulting combinations *True Positive (TP), True Negative (TN), False Positive (FP), and False Negative (FN).* In our context, the

TABLE III: NUMBER OF SIMILAR PAIRS ABOVE 10 PERCENT INCREMENTAL THRESHOLDS

	Low			*High*		
threshold	both singleton	one singleton	none singleton	both singleton	one singleton	none singleton
0.0	26335	52900	26335	26335	52900	26335
0.1	4843	389	31	22628	21859	7950
0.2	1444	4	4	10395	1630	600
0.3	372	0	1	3737	118	73
0.4	135	0	1	1589	9	28
0.5	73	0	0	669	0	16
0.6	43	0	0	289	0	8
0.7	32	0	0	153	0	1
0.8	28	0	0	95	0	1
0.9	27	0	0	63	0	0
1.0	25	0	0	30	0	0

TABLE IV: SUB SETS OF THE DATA SET AND THE AMOUNT OF THEIR EXCLUSIVE PATHS

	# paths only in		# paths in all		# paths seen
	singletons	non-singletons (P_{ex})	singletons (P_{in})	non-singletons	in both sets
trimmed	0	8	12	0	279
not trimmed	4644	12813	12	0	1996

classes mean: *TP*: prediction and ground truth agree on singleton; *TN*: prediction and ground truth agree on non-singleton; *FP*: prediction says singleton but it is not a singleton; and *FN*: predict says non-singleton but it is a singleton. To evaluate the performance of our classification of unseen samples we stick to the metrics of a confusion matrix used for the evaluation of Machine Learning (ML) models. Table V shows the results for the conducted experiments. Calculations of *Precision* also known as *Positive Predictive Value (PPV)*, *Recall* also known as *True Positive Rate (TPR)*, *Accuracy (ACC)*, and *F1* are also calculated. A general remark is that the files were not changed or preprocessed. In the case of data set *java-singleton*, we isolated one class per code sample, contrarily those files used for the prediction are still untouched and possibly contain multiple classes.

B. Discussion

We have seen that abstractions produced by samples of various origins (different projects) carrying the same design pattern still carry a certain degree of similarity on the different levels of abstraction introduced in this paper. In terms of formulating the shared concepts, we were able to formulate a set of paths included in all samples and exclude a set of paths that we have only seen in other implementations that do not contain the same design pattern in the first place. The inclusion set P_{in} contains twelve paths, and the minimum number of paths seen in the set of singletons (see Table II) is only 17. This allows drawing the conclusions that at least one sample contains almost the bare minimum needed to implement a singleton in java.

TABLE V: RESULTS OF THE PREDICTION TASKS

	TP	TN	FP	FN	TPR	PPV	ACC	F1
High incl.	12	1914	13	0	1.0	.48	.993	.649
High	8	1919	8	4	$.\overline{6}$	.5	.994	.571
Low	12	13	0	0	1.0	1.0	1.0	1.0

The exclusion set P_{ex} serves another important purpose, as it helps to explicitly describe what should not be part of the concept. In the case of the conducted evaluation, we reduced the exclusion set by trimming all paths that were in less than five percent of the samples, which allowed us to reduce the set from 12813 to only eight paths. We argue that this is useful because of the rather small sample size. We have not found another approach that similarly describes a concept by explicitly stating what is not part of the desired concept. Paths contained in P_{ex} were contrary to the definition of a singleton, as they contain paths for *Public Constructors*, and paths for creating new objects in the return statement of a method (which would bypass the singleton object, if it would be the *getInstance* method).

Also, the approach of the formulation of such a shared concept is flexible and adapts to the considered samples, and the more the samples share, the more is included. As the paths are interpretable, the abstraction levels introduced in this work also allow a formulation of such shared concepts from scratch, or to use only one example as a template to start with.

Both runs on $High$ have a PPV around 0.5, while the TPR is higher, not making use of the exclusion paths P_{ex}. The ACC of both approaches is also nearly identical at 0.99. Caused by the data having a lot of *Negative* cases, in which both approaches are good at predicting. By comparing both runs, it is indicating that $High$ lowers the prediction of singleton (TP and FP) while introducing FN. The last part of the evaluation has been performed on Low. In this case, we introduced indices to the paths in P_{in}. We then aligned the indices of the samples, according to a valid permutation. The results have a PPV, TPR, and ACC of 1. This classification task was only performed on the 25 samples predicted as *TRUE* on the most permissive other approach (*High incl.*). As of two main reasons, (i) the computation needed to find a subgraph isomorphism is NP-complete [16], and (ii) the previous check on $High$ for all P_{in} excludes all the other samples for not having all the needed paths. By knowing not all paths are present in the other samples (regardless of indices) it is not possible to find indices for those samples so that all paths are included afterward.

In terms of the classification performed, we have shown predictions with simple models, checking the exact inclusion and exclusion of specific paths on the $High$ and the same thing (after the computational intense subgraph isomorphism checking) on Low, with a perfect result as a reward. The prediction on $High$ is prone to overestimate the concept to be included, which is indicated by a precision around 0.5 for the not preprocessed unseen samples. Nevertheless, $High$ serves a valuable purpose in filtering the relevant samples to further look at Low.

C. Limitations

Although the approach introduced gives promising results in terms of the stated RQs, we have encountered some limitations on which we want to elaborate.

The design pattern chosen is rather simple in terms of the variety the implementation offers. Looking at more complex structures (e.g., using general parts and specific refined parts could implement those as interfaces or (abstract) classes), in terms of the shown abstraction levels this would lead to not being reflected in P_{in} as of the current approach on building the inclusion set.

Assigning index-values to the shared concept Low was the only time (except the labeling) we relied on understanding the concept (of the singleton). To address that, the indexing can be seen as the maximum common subgraph problem [17](being NP-Hard [16]). We do not have an implementation of this in our prototype.

V. RELATED WORK

A similar approach to the one we propose is code2vec [18], [19], also working with an abstraction based on a set of paths. The main difference is the structure of the extracted path. All pairwise paths between the leaf nodes are examined and limited to a maximum number and length. They define the path-context by a triplet $< x_s, p, x_t >$, where x_s is the start leaf, x_t is the target leaf, and p the path between these nodes with the additional information whether a traversal takes place upwards towards the root element or downwards in the tree. The approach is presented here all paths from each leaf to the root are taken into account. Another limitation of code2vec is the abstraction context, which is one method. They argue that the order of source code statements is not relevant, valid for this scope and the defined task. But as shown in [20], the relation between source code elements for higher concepts (like classes) is essential to perform structural or behavioral related tasks. As shown in [21] another limitation of code2vec is its sensitivity to naming. For tasks like those described in code2vec, where names of methods are predicted, names are of course essential, but for the extraction of abstract concepts the uncertainty of the correct name is too high.

Yarahmadi et al. [20] have conducted an extensive and systematic literature review on how design patterns can be detected in code and therefore abstract the code to perform this task. The main findings of this study relevant to this paper are: Many of the approaches have been tested and evaluated only on small data sets or on limited code samples. The principle in almost all approaches that were reviewed is to reduce the search space by abstraction. Most approaches were limited in their ability to recognize different types of patterns. Another problem of many approaches is to detect different variants of a pattern. To make this possible, ML methods are often used. However, these methods require good data preprocessing because it is not possible to decide in a general way which parts should be selected for learning. A common approach to this problem is, as implemented in [22], a semi-automatic approach in which a human takes over feedback or labeling.

Another principle often used in addition to using the syntactic concepts of programming languages is to analyze the identifiers (e.g., classes, methods, or variable names) using natural language processing techniques [23], [24]. In Schindler et al. [24] demonstrated that these methods are well suited for project-specific domain models but not for identifying general patterns. Natural language identifiers can be an indication but not a robust criterion. An example on how the AST is able to be enriched by additional features, e.g., by using ML, is described in [25] and [26].

In addition, tools and frameworks should also be mentioned, which could also be applied, though in part with restrictions. For example, jQAssistent [27] is a tool that transfers the AST into a Neo4j graph database, offers the possibility of manually enriching this graph with further information, and then using the query-language Cypher to define concepts and identify them in the graph. In contrast to the approach presented in this paper, a query needs to be formulated covering the concept for which the sample should be retrieved.

ArchUnit [28], Structure101 [29], and Dependometer [30] are based on the same principle of formulating rules that are checked automatically afterward. However, the creation and management of rules is costly with the increasing complexity of the concept, requires substantial expert knowledge. All of the mentioned approaches do not assist in expressing rules applying to a given set of samples.

The major problem in this kind of approach and any other approach based on a specific formal language is that it is difficult to define the concrete rules describing a pattern correctly. Rasool et al. [31] describe it as a lack of standard specification for design patterns.

The field of code clone detection is related to the approach presented in this paper since the input data is identical. Wang et al. [32], four types of code clone detection are characterized, (i) syntactically identical code fragments, (ii) syntactically identical except names and literal values, (iii) syntactically similar fragments that differ in some statements but can be transformed to each other by simple operations and (iv) syntactically dissimilar code fragments but sharing the same functionality. In contrast to code clone detection, we do neither want to find syntactically identical fragments (i)-(iii) nor functionally identical ones (iv). Because of the domain-specific adaptation, we are not interested in finding direct copies.

VI. Conclusion and Future Work

We have shown how to extract the essence of a shared concept, driven by available implementations, so that the formulation is interpretable by humans. Moreover, what we have not found in the literature, is the formulation of what should explicitly not be part of the implementation. Future work planned includes addressing the stated limitations and collecting a high quality and high quantity data set of different design patterns, including also different variants of a pattern.

The abstraction presented in this paper produces a set of paths from a semantically aggregated syntax graph. We plan on utilizing the shown approach as a preprocessing step in the direction of ML techniques. For example, to train classifier or cluster samples to identify variants or the inner parts of a pattern, e.g., roles.

In Herold et al. [33] and Knieke et al. [34], a holistic approach is described to mitigate architecture degradation using ML. For such approaches, it is essential to have relevant training data available and to understand which expected patterns are not present in the implementation. This would also be a use case supported by the method presented here.

References

[1] E. Gamma, R. Helm, R. Johnson, and J. Vlissides, *Design patterns: Elements of reusable object-oriented software*, 2nd ed., ser. Addison-Wesley professional computing series. Boston: Addison-Wesley, 1997.

[2] J. Coplien, *Software Patterns*. SIGS Books & Multimedia, 1996.

[3] K. Bergner, A. Rausch, and M. Sihling, *Using UML for Modeling a Distributed Java Application*, 1997. [Online]. Available: http://citeseerx.ist.psu.edu/viewdoc/summary?doi=10.1.1.42.6797

[4] G. Sunyé, A. Le Guennec, and J.-M. Jézéquel, "Design patterns application in uml," in *European Conference on Object-Oriented Programming*, 2000, pp. 44–62.

[5] S. Hussain, J. Keung, and A. A. Khan, "The effect of gang-of-four design patterns usage on design quality attributes," in *2017 IEEE International Conference on Software Quality, Reliability and Security (QRS)*. IEEE, 2017, pp. 263–273.

[6] C. Deiters and A. Rausch, "Assuring architectural properties during compositional architecture design," in *International Conference on Software Composition*. Springer, 2011, pp. 141–148.

[7] M. Paixao, J. Krinke, D. Han, C. Ragkhitwetsagul, and M. Harman, "Are developers aware of the architectural impact of their changes?" in *2017 32nd IEEE/ACM International Conference on Automated Software Engineering (ASE)*, 2017, pp. 95–105.

[8] M. Schindler and S. Lawrenz, "Community-driven design in software engineering," in *Proceedings of the 19th International Conference on Software Engineering Research & Practice, Las Vegas, NV, USA*, 2021.

[9] M. L. Scott, *Programming language pragmatics*, 4th ed. Amsterdam and Boston and Heidelberg and London and New York and Oxford and Paris and San Diego and San Francisco and Singapore and Sydney and Tokyo: Morgan Kaufmann/Elsevier, 2016.

[10] N. Chomsky and D. Lightfoot, *Syntactic structures*, 2nd ed., ser. A Mouton classic. Berlin: Mouton de Gruyter, 2002.

[11] N. Chomsky, "Three models for the description of language," *IEEE Transactions on Information Theory*, vol. 2, no. 3, pp. 113–124, 1956.

[12] A. V. Aho, M. S. Lam, R. Sethi, and J. D. Ullman, *Compilers: Principles, techniques, & tools*, 2nd ed. Boston: Pearson Addison Wesley, 2007.

[13] J. Niere, J. P. Wadsack, and L. Wendehals, "Handling large search space in pattern-based reverse engineering," in *11th IEEE International Workshop on Program Comprehension, 2003*. IEEE, 2003, pp. 274–279.

[14] A. Rajaraman and J. D. Ullman, "Data mining," in *Mining of Massive Datasets*, A. Rajaraman and J. D. Ullman, Eds. Cambridge: Cambridge University Press, 2011, pp. 1–17.

[15] P-mart pattern-like micro-architecture repository. [retrieved: 03, 2022]. [Online]. Available: https://www.ptidej.net/tools/designpatterns/index_html

[16] M. R. Garey and D. S. Johnson, *Computers and intractability: A guide to the theory of NP-completeness*, ser. A series of books in the mathematical sciences. New York u.a: Freeman, 1979.

[17] V. Kann, "On the approximability of the maximum common subgraph problem," in *Annual Symposium on Theoretical Aspects of Computer Science*. Springer, 1992, pp. 375–388.

[18] U. Alon, M. Zilberstein, O. Levy, and E. Yahav, "A general path-based representation for predicting program properties," in *Proceedings of the 39th ACM SIGPLAN Conference on Programming Language Design and Implementation*, ser. PLDI 2018. New York, NY, USA: Association for Computing Machinery, 2018, p. 404–419.

[19] ——, "code2vec: Learning distributed representations of code," *Proceedings of the ACM on Programming Languages*, vol. 3, no. POPL, pp. 1–29, 2019.

[20] H. Yarahmadi and S. M. H. Hasheminejad, "Design pattern detection approaches: a systematic review of the literature," *Artificial Intelligence Review*, vol. 53, no. 8, pp. 5789–5846, 2020.

[21] R. Compton, E. Frank, P. Patros, and A. Koay, "Embedding java classes with code2vec: Improvements from variable obfuscation," in *Proceedings of the 17th International Conference on Mining Software Repositories*, 2020, pp. 243–253.

[22] G. Rasool, I. Philippow, and P. Mäder, "Design pattern recovery based on annotations," *Advances in Engineering Software*, vol. 41, no. 4, pp. 519–526, 2010.

[23] P. Warintarawej, M. Huchard, M. Lafourcade, A. Laurent, and P. Pompidor, "Software understanding: Automatic classification of software identifiers," *Intelligent Data Analysis*, vol. 19, no. 4, pp. 761–778, 2015.

[24] M. Schindler, A. Rausch, and O. Fox, "Clustering source code elements by semantic similarity using wikipedia," in *Proceedings of 4th International Workshop on Realizing Artificial Intelligence Synergies in Software Engineering (RAISE)*, 2015, pp. 13–18.

[25] J. He, C.-C. Lee, V. Raychev, and M. Vechev, "Learning to find naming issues with big code and small supervision," in *2021 42nd ACM SIGPLAN International Conference on Programming Language Design and Implementation (PLDI '21)*. ACM, 2021, pp. 1–16.

[26] M. Schindler and A. Rausch, "Architectural concepts and their evolution made explicit by examples," in *ADAPTIVE 2019, The Eleventh International Conference on Adaptive and Self-Adaptive Systems and Applications*, vol. 11, 2019, pp. 38–43.

[27] jqassistant — your software . your structures . your rules. [retrieved: 03, 2022]. [Online]. Available: https://jqassistant.org

[28] Unit test your java architecture - archunit. [retrieved: 03, 2022]. [Online]. Available: https://www.archunit.org

[29] Structure101 software architecture development environment (ade). [retrieved: 03, 2022]. [Online]. Available: https://structure101.com

[30] Dependometer. [retrieved: 03, 2022]. [Online]. Available: https://github.com/dheraclio/dependometer

[31] G. Rasool and D. Streitfdert, "A survey on design pattern recovery techniques," *International Journal of Computer Science Issues (IJCSI)*, vol. 8, no. 6, p. 251, 2011.

[32] W. Wang, G. Li, B. Ma, X. Xia, and Z. Jin, "Detecting code clones with graph neural network and flow-augmented abstract syntax tree," in *2020 IEEE 27th International Conference on Software Analysis, Evolution and Reengineering (SANER)*. IEEE, 2020, pp. 261–271.

[33] S. Herold, C. Knieke, M. Schindler, and A. Rausch, "Towards improving software architecture degradation mitigation by machine learning," in *ADAPTIVE 2020, The Twelfth International Conference on Adaptive and Self-Adaptive Systems and Applications*, 2020, pp. 36–39.

[34] C. Knieke, A. Rausch, and M. Schindler, "Tackling software architecture erosion: Joint architecture and implementation repairing by a knowledge-based approach," in *2021 IEEE/ACM International Workshop on Automated Program Repair (APR)*. IEEE, 6/1/2021 - 6/1/2021, pp. 19–20.

Usage of Machine Learning for Subtopology Detection in Wire and Arc Additive Manufacturing

Dimitri Bratzel, Stefan Wittek, Andreas Rausch
Institute of Software and Systems Engineering
Technische Universität Clausthal
Clausthal-Zellerfeld, Germany
email: switt@tu-clausthal.de

Kai Treutler, Tobias Gehling, Volker Wesling
Institute of Welding and Machining
Technische Universität Clausthal
Clausthal-Zellerfeld, Germany
email: office@isaf.tu-clausthal.de

Abstract - **In additive manufacturing, knowledge of the geometry of the weld seam is crucial for the quality of the component. This is especially true for Wire and Arc Additive Manufacturing (WAAM) based on Gas Metal Arc Welding (GMAW). The length of the free wire electrode ("stickout") should be almost constant during the entire manufacturing process. In additive manufacturing, it is also important to recognize height differences that occur during the process and to compensate for them by adjusting the process parameters in order to achieve a uniform build rate across the component cross-section, as geometric irregularities tend to be amplified by multiple layers. Furthermore, process disturbances can lead to locally altered seam properties. To counteract these problems, the presented investigations show to what extent such geometric irregularities can be detected in-situ from the existing process variables welding current and voltage. This makes it possible to dispense with the use of additional measurement technology. In our experiments, we simulated these height differences during multilayer welding by means of defined unevenness on the substrate plate. With the help of a Long Short Memory Neuronal Network (LSTM), the height information is determined indirectly during the process only via welding current and voltage. It is shown that this approach could be used to control the process. Furthermore, it is shown that this approach can reliably detect geometry errors and determine the height information with high accuracy, even if the process parameters are changed between training and validation.**

Keywords: WAAM, Welding, GMAW, Machine Learning, Long Short-Term Memory, topology detection

I. INTRODUCTION

In order to ensure consistent weld seam quality, even in automated welding processes, with slightly changing geometric boundary conditions, a wide variety of sensor-based detection systems are currently being used. Among other things, the shape of the seam is detected by laser-based systems, usually using the light-sectioning method, to enable good seam tracking. On the other hand, the size of the melt pool is observed by optical systems [1]. An overview of the current state of research on monitoring and control of additive manufacturing is given in [2–4]. In addition to the dimension of the molten pool, conclusions can also be drawn here about the cooling of the weld seam or solidification. This not only allows the geometry of the weld to be determined, but also allows material properties to be specifically adjusted via the cooling. Thus, the monitoring of the welding process represents a multi-criteria task, especially in the case of a weld-property orientation in additive manufacturing. One approach to solve such a multi-criteria task in advance has been shown by Ehlers et. al. in [5]. Due to increasingly complex applications of common welding processes, such as additive manufacturing, the task is also becoming more complex and sensory monitoring is becoming more important [6–9].

Complex, multi-criteria tasks can be solved using various artificial intelligence methods and, most importantly, can be computed in real time. Real-time computability is one of the main requirements for in-situ welding process monitoring and control, especially to be able to realize a material property oriented welding sequence as, e.g. in [5][10]. In these works, the cooling time between metallurgically important temperatures was used as a controlled variable, such as the $t_{8/5}$-time concept to keep the material properties within a desired range.

In the following, a way to determine the geometry of the substrate for a weld bead based on welding current and voltage using artificial intelligence is presented. The aim is to derive further parameters from the existing process parameters without measuring them directly. This opens up the perspective of a material property- or geometry-oriented welding process control for metal inert gas welding.

The results presented in this paper were discussed in German language in [11].

A. Machine learning in welding and WAAM

The accurate prediction of the complex WAAM Process using numerical models is challenging and as of today, there exists no such model that could reliably predict the outcome of the process, outside vary narrow experimental frameworks. Even if such a model would exist, the required computation time may easy make it impractical for the online monitoring tasks addressed in this paper. This is the reason why we focus on machine learned models, which can be trained, only using captured inline process data and can be inferred very fast, so that the online approach becomes viable. A number of other authors have committed works tackling this topic.

One major direction of the works lays in the prediction of some aspects of the overall outcome of the process based on parameters of the whole run. Most of this works rely on Artificial Neuronal Networks (ANN). One such approach predicts the mean width and height of the weld based on the mean current and voltage using fixed feed and tool speeds [12]. Another approach relies on a set of process parameters including energy and feed speed, as well as tool speed [13]. In [14], this approach is even extend to not only predict the over all geometry but also the distortion that may occur. In [15], a hybrid approach is presented, using the ANN to predict the temperature distribution of the weld and then use this as an input for an FEM model to come to the stress and strain of the underlaying metal sheet. Another parameter of the resulting weld that can be predicted this way is the surface roughness [16][17]. Common to all of these approaches is, that all of them use simple feed forward architectures to do regression from process parameters to outcome quantities. This has little in common with the idea of an inline approach where every measured value is directly used to predict some hidden value, such as the sub topology.

There are some works, mainly from the point of view of a control engineer, that forester such an inline view. In [18], for example, ANN are used to predict the temperature of a top layer based on the temperature of the layer underneath it. Other approaches are focused on online image recognition and the corresponding convolutional neuronal network architectures to interpreted inline imagery. In [19], image recognition on IR cameras is used to preprocess the obtained images to than measure meld pool geometry using classical methods. Another example application for image recognition lays in detecting humps and valleys in the weld using a HDR camera sensing the process [20]. In [21], a very different approach is used. Here reinforcement learning is employed in order to control the geometry using inter layer scans of the top layer as an input.

While the results of this are promising, they require to bring new sensory into the process, which on the one hand, may be costly, and become an additional source of system failure. Additionally, none of the presented approaches treats the measured sensory data as a time series. This is due to the architectures for the neuronal networks chosen. This paper overcomes this shortage by using a network architecture suitable for this task. In the past, Long Short Term Memory neuronal networks (LSTM) have proven to be very suitable for predictions based on time series data [22].

While ANNs do stateless regression form a domain X to an image space Y, LSTM are able to internally keep a state based on the last observer sensory values X and perform a prediction of Y based on these past observations. In section II the used materials and methods for the welding experiments carried out and the used neuronal network will be described. Followed by Section III presenting the results and Section IV in which the results are discussed.

II. MATERIALS AND METHODS

To record the training and comparison data for the neural networks used, a "Fronius TransPuls Synergic 4000 CMT" welding power source was coupled with a robot from Kuka as an automated motion system and equipped with a laser triangulation displacement sensor type optoNCDT 1420 from MICRO-EPSILON for distance measurement. The current and voltage signals, as well as the distance measurement values were recorded with a "Scope Corder DL750" from Yokogawa. To create defined height differences in the substrate, the substrate plate was provided with elevations and grooves, Figure 1.

The grooves are 4 mm deep and the elevations 4 mm high. The grooves and elevations have an angle of 90°. These selected defined changes are in the upper range of typical seam irregularities and seam defects. Depending on the choice of process adjustment variables, an GMA-weld can have a height of 1mm to 9mm and a width between 2.5mm and 20mm.

A total of ten welding tests were carried out. Welding was carried out across the tests as follows:

Welding consumable:	ISO14341-A-G 4Mo
Wire electrode diameter:	1.2 mm
Shielding gas:	82% Ar / 18% CO_2
Welding speed:	55 cm/min
Stick-out:	15 mm
Base material:	S355

The wire feeds, the resulting average current and voltage values and the set process can be taken from Table 1. In addition to different wire feeds, both the standard and the in-pulse welding process were used.

The experimental setup is sketched in Figure 2.a, with the welding direction out of the image plane. To measure the changes in distance between the displacement sensor and the substrate material, the arc of light was shielded from the sensor. Figure 2b shows a sketch of the substrate plate used.

Figure 1: Side view of the base plate

TABLE 1: EXPERIMENTAL CONDITIONS

Run. Nr.	Wire feed speed	Current	Voltage	Welding Mode
1	4,5	93	17,0	Impulse
2	4,5	93	17,0	Impulse
3	4,5	93	17,1	Impulse
4	4,8	136	14,5	Standard
5	4,8	136	14,5	Standard
6	4,8	136	14,6	Standard
7	7,0	171	16,2	Standard
8	1,7	37	14,7	Impulse
9	1,7	37	14,2	Impulse
10	1,7	37	15,2	Impulse

A. *Methodology in the use of artificial intelligence*

The collected raw data of the 10 tests consist of the measured quantities: voltage [volts], current [amps] and distance [mm]. The measurement data of tests 3, 9 and 10 had to be discarded due to recording errors. Voltage and current are the input variables, with the help of which height differences should be indirectly predicted. To eliminate extreme outliers, a filter was applied. For the distance, values larger than 190 mm and smaller than 160 mm were removed. For voltage, values greater than 40 V and less than 10 V were eliminated. Furthermore, the distance measurement exhibits noise that occurs at regular intervals, with an amplitude of about +/-4 mm and a period of oscillation of a few milliseconds. Since the defined geometry irregularities are in a comparable order of magnitude, it is necessary to clean this noise to obtain good labels for training the LSTM. Furthermore, the input quantities have voltage and current typical characteristics with very high amplitudes and extreme values, which were identified as measurement errors. All three quantities were preprocessed in two steps. In the first step, the moving average method was used with a triangular weighting and a window width of 10,000 measurement points. In the second step, averaging was applied, reducing the total number of measurement points from about 3 million per experiment to about 900 to 1,000 measurement points. This eliminated most of the periodic oscillations and outliers. Figure 3 shows all three measured variables. For the illustration, the values were scaled in preparation for the training. By reducing the number of measurement points, the scaling of the x-axis (previously time) is lost. Only the sequence of data points is shown. It can be seen that there is a correlation between the input variables (current and voltage) and the output variable (distance).

For each experiment, a model with the same network architecture was trained. As a result, seven models were available, each of which was trained on one experiment.

The input values are stored as a three-dimensional tensor, whereby a label with a corresponding distance measurement is available for a series of data. During the learning process, the neural network looks at the past 50 values (the time window chosen in this analysis) and deduces the current distance from the torch to the workpiece. Since the input is a sequence of current and voltage values and only one distance value is to be predicted, a funnel-shaped architecture of the LSTM was chosen. The models were implemented in Python

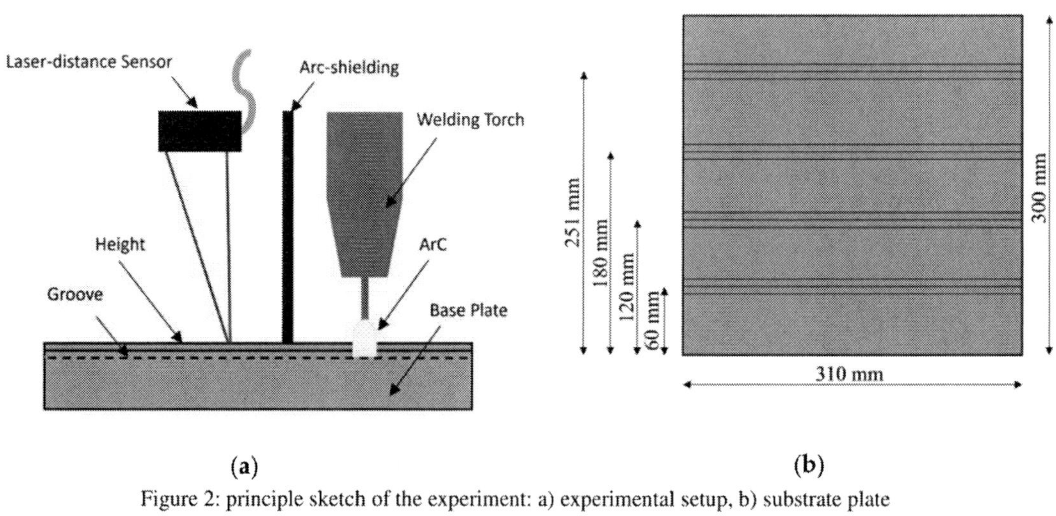

Figure 2: principle sketch of the experiment: a) experimental setup, b) substrate plate

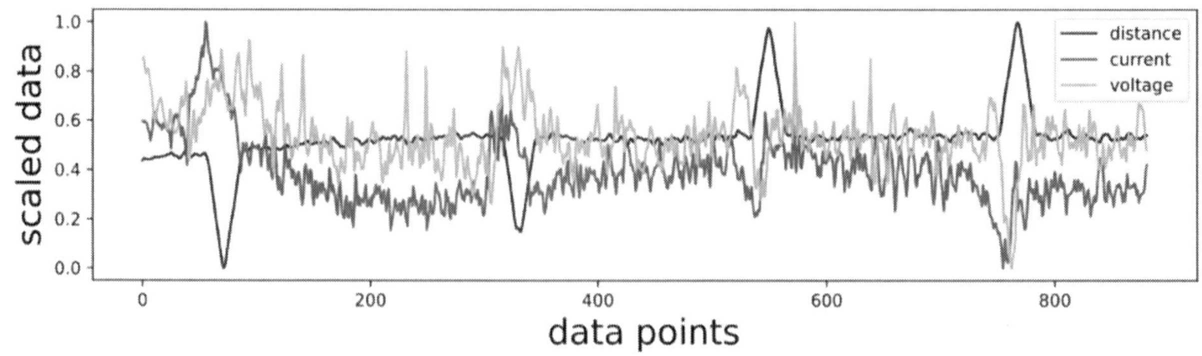

Figure 3: Scaled and preprocessed measured values of experiment 1

using the KERAS framework. The corresponding parameterization of the network with two layers and neurons: Layer_1 = 50 and Layer_2 = 20. There is only one neuron in the output layer, this one carries the value of the distance. The "Mean Squared Error" serves as the "loss function" or cost function and "ADAM" was chosen as the method of stochastic optimization. Only for experiment 7 a bias regulator (L2=0,1) was used additionally, because the model showed typical signs of overfitting. All models were trained over 500 epochs, with a batch size of 60.

III. Results

Within the experiments, the first two thirds were used as training data. On the last third, the model was tested (see Figure 4). In addition, the generalization of the models between the experiments was tested. This was only successful between trials with the same procedure (impulse or standard). In each case, the models were applied to an entirely different data set. Figure 5 shows the Mean Absolute Deviation (MAE) of the models (rows) when applied to the different tests (columns) for the tests with impulse (a) and standard (b) methods. This can be interpreted as the mean deviation of the predicted profile from the actual profile. The maximum deviation is 0.29 mm, the minimum 0.18 mm.

The models perform differently if used to predict profiles of experiments not used for training. The mean absolute error form most cases (except for experiment 8), remains well below one millimeter, even in this cross-experiment setup.

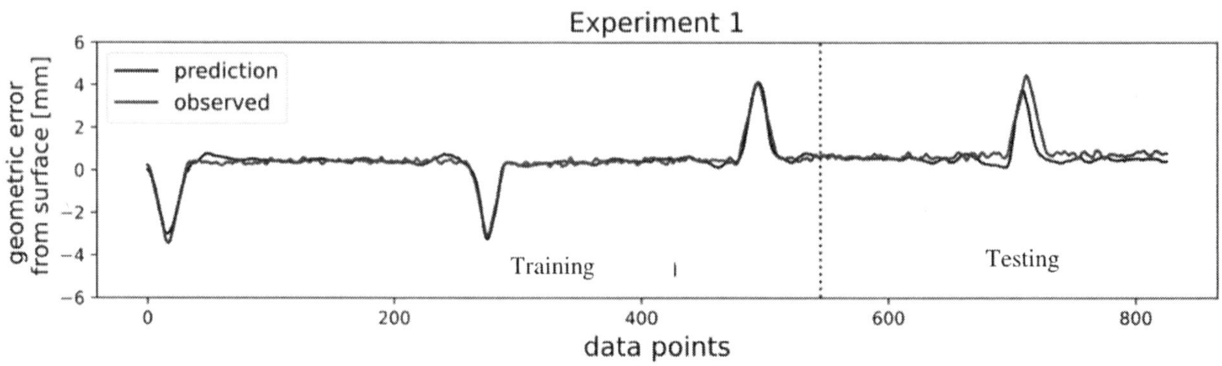

Figure 4: Prediction accuracy in the training and test area, experiment 1

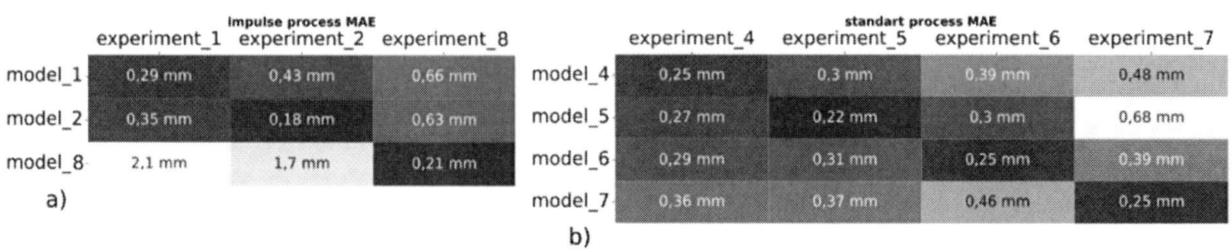

Figure 5: Mean Absolute Deviation of all tests

IV. Discussion

In the presented work, it was shown that the use of neural networks allows to estimate the substrate topography in GMA-welding with high accuracy. Furthermore, it was shown that even with a small number of training experiments and a limited database for different process variants, small deviations of the prediction from the actual value in the lower tenth of a millimeter range could be achieved. The work presented is promising. Therefore, they are to be extended to real welding tests and to the application in additive manufacturing using larger data bases and further process parameters such as the light emitted by the arc, as well as the melt pool size and the temperature distribution. Although the chosen LSTM network architecture proved to be capable for the application described, additional comparative experiments using a wide array of methods is needed.

V. Conclusion

The work conducted in this paper shows that the usage of a neuronal network for the prediction of the stick-out and/or the geometry of the topologies beneath the actual weld seam is possible. It was possible to generate the necessary database for teaching the network in only a few experiments. Even this relatively low number of experiments resulted in a prediction accuracy that is sufficiently precise for the application. As mentioned above one obvious direction for further work lays in transferring the approach from a single layer welding experiment to actual additive manufacturing in multiple layers. Another direction is to close the loop by implementing a controller based on the predicted subtopology to compensate errors. This is by no means trivial, since the control algorithm itself would interfere with voltage and current, thusly challenging the prediction capability of the network.

REFERENCES

[1] A. Richter, T. Gehling, K. Treutler, V. Wesling, and C. Rembe, "Real-time measurement of temperature and volume of the weld pool in wire-arc additive manufacturing," *Measurement: Sensors* 2021, *17*, pp. 100060-100069, doi:10.1016/j.measen.2021.100060.

[2] K. Treutler and V. Wesling, "The Current State of Research of Wire Arc Additive Manufacturing (WAAM): A Review," *Applied Sciences* 2021, *11*, pp. 8619-8625, doi:10.3390/app11188619.

[3] S. Singh, S. K. Sharma, and D. W. Rathod, "A review on process planning strategies and challenges of WAAM," *Materials Today: Proceedings* 2021, *47*, pp. 6564-6575, doi:10.1016/j.matpr.2021.02.632.

[4] C. Xia, et al., "A review on wire arc additive manufacturing: Monitoring, control and a framework of automated system," *Journal of Manufacturing Systems* 2020, *57*, pp. 31-45, doi:10.1016/j.jmsy.2020.08.008.

[5] R. Ehlers, K. Treutler, and V. Wesling, "SAT Solving with Fragmented Hamiltonian Path Constraints for Wire Arc Additive Manufacturing," In *Theory and Applications of Satisfiability Testing - SAT 2020*; Pulina, Hofmann, Eds.; Springer International Publishing: [S.l.], 2020; pp. 492-500, ISBN 978-3-030-51824-0.

[6] A. Chabot, M. Rauch, and J.-Y. Hascoët, "Towards a multi-sensor monitoring methodology for AM metallic processes," *Weld World* 2019, *63*, pp. 759-769, doi:10.1007/s40194-019-00705-4.

[7] C. Halisch, T. Radel, D. Tyralla, and T. Seefeld, "Measuring the melt pool size in a wire arc additive manufacturing process using a high dynamic range two-colored pyrometric camera," *Weld World* 2020, *64*, pp. 1349-1356, doi:10.1007/s40194-020-00892-5.

[8] X. Wang, A. Wang, and Y. Li. „An online surface height measurement method for GTAW-based additive manufacturing," *Weld World* 2020, *64*, pp. 11-20, doi:10.1007/s40194-019-00813-1.

[9] A. Waqas, X. Qin, J. Xiong, H. Wang, and C. Zheng, „Optimization of Process Parameters to Improve the Effective Area of Deposition in GMAW-Based Additive Manufacturing and its Mechanical and Microstructural Analysis," *Metals* 2019, *9*, pp. 775-798, doi:10.3390/met9070775.

[10] K. Treutler, S. Kamper, M. Leicher, T. Bick, and V. Wesling. "Multi-Material Design in Welding Arc Additive Manufacturing," *Metals* 2019, *9*, pp. 809-823, doi:10.3390/met9070809.

[11] D. Bratzel, S. Wittek, A. Rausch, K. Treutler, T. Gehling, and V. Wesling. „Using AI Methods for Subtopology Detection in MSG-Welding" i.o. „Nutzung von KI-Methoden zur Geometriedetektion beim MSG-Schweißen," In *Tagungsband 4. Symposium Materialtechnik*; Clausthaler Zentrum für Materialtechnik, Ed.; Shaker Verlag: Düren, 2021; pp. 127–136, ISBN 978-3-8440-8021-6.

[12] G. O. Barrionuevo, S. Rios, S. W. Williams, and J. Andres Ramos-Grez, "Comparative Evaluation of Machine Learning Regressors for the Layer Geometry Prediction in Wire arc Additive manufacturing," In *2021 IEEE 12th International Conference on Mechanical and Intelligent Manufacturing Technologies (ICMIMT)*; IEEE, 2021; pp. 186-190.

[13] J. Deng, Y. Xu, Z. Zuo, Z. Hou, and S. Chen, "Bead Geometry Prediction for Multi-layer and Multi-bead Wire and Arc Additive Manufacturing Based on XGBoost,"

Transactions on Intelligent Welding Manufacturing; Springer, Singapore, 2019; pp. 125-135.

[14] C. Wacker, et al. , "Geometry and Distortion Prediction of Multiple Layers for Wire Arc Additive Manufacturing with Artificial Neural Networks," *Applied Sciences* 2021, *11*, pp. 4694-4709 , doi:10.3390/app11104694.

[15] Q. Wu, T. Mukherjee, A. De, and T. DebRoy, "Residual stresses in wire-arc additive manufacturing – Hierarchy of influential variables," *Additive Manufacturing* 2020, *35*, pp. 101355-101327, doi:10.1016/j.addma.2020.101355.

[16] C. Xia, et al., "Modelling and prediction of surface roughness in wire arc additive manufacturing using machine learning," *J Intell Manuf* 2021, pp. 1-16, doi:10.1007/s10845-020-01725-4.

[17] A. Yaseer and H. Chen, "Machine learning based layer roughness modeling in robotic additive manufacturing," *Journal of Manufacturing Processes* 2021, *70*, pp. 543-552, doi:10.1016/j.jmapro.2021.08.056.

[18] P. K. Nalajam and R. Varadarajan, "A Hybrid Deep Learning Model for Layer-Wise Melt Pool Temperature Forecasting in Wire-Arc Additive Manufacturing Process," *IEEE Access* 2021, *9*, pp. 100652-100664, doi:10.1109/access.2021.3097177.

[19] Y. Wang, et al., "Active disturbance rejection control of layer width in wire arc additive manufacturing based on deep learning," *Journal of Manufacturing Processes* 2021, *67*, pp. 364-375, doi:10.1016/j.jmapro.2021.05.005.

[20] C. Lee, G. Seo, D. B. Kim, M. Kim, and J.-H. Shin, "Development of Defect Detection AI Model for Wire + Arc Additive Manufacturing Using High Dynamic Range Images," *Applied Sciences* 2021, *11*, pp. 7541-7560, doi:10.3390/app11167541.

[21] A. G. Dharmawan, Y. Xiong, S. Foong, and G. Song Soh. "A Model-Based Reinforcement Learning and Correction Framework for Process Control of Robotic Wire Arc Additive Manufacturing," In *2020 IEEE International Conference on Robotics and Automation (ICRA)*; IEEE, 2020; pp. 4030-4036.

[22] F. A. Gers, J. Schmidhuber, and F. Cummins. "Learning to forget: continual prediction with LSTM," *Neural Computation* 2000, *12*, pp. 2451-2471, doi:10.1162/089976600300015015.

Towards A Data Marketplace Ecosystem
Blueprint For A Community-Driven Data Marketplace

Sebastian Lawrenz, Priyanka Sharma, Andreas Rausch
Clausthal University of Technology, Center for Digital Technologies
Wallstraße 06
Goslar, Germany
email: {sebastian.lawrenz | priyanka.sharma | andreas.rausch}@tu-clausthal.de

Abstract— **The amount of data generation has been increasing exponentially over the last decades. The reasons for this amount of data are pretty similar: The evolution of technology, as well as new technologies, such as the Internet of things or artificial intelligence, as well as data-driven business models. However, the profiteers of the data boom are few players, like big tech companies. Small- and medium-size companies do not have access to the same amount of data and thus cannot benefit from the data boom and adapt their business models. This paper presents the concept of a data marketplace ecosystem to overcome the inbalance between big tech companies and these smaller companies. In comparison to other data marketplaces, our proposal is entirely community-driven. Instead of a single authority or player, it is developed and controlled by a community. The concept is closely related to software ecosystems and adaptive and open systems. The paper presents a blueprint of such an ecosystem based on blockchain technology and smart contracts, discusses the related state of the art, and reflects critically on the results.**

Keywords- Blockchain; Data; Data marketplaces; Community; Data ecosystem; Open platforms, Data Trading.

I. INTRODUCTION

Over the last decades, the amount of data generation has been exponentially increasing, driven by new technologies like the Internet of Things (IoT) and Artificial Intelligence (AI) [1]. In 2020, people created 1.7 MB of data every second, and by the end of 2020, 44 zettabytes made up the entire digital universe. This amount of data means there are 40 times more bytes than stars in the observable universe!

Data is generated and collected in such a massive amount is pretty simple: Data has become the oil of the 21st Century [3]. Data is the fuel for new business models that are common for the most valuable companies in 2021, like Amazon, Apple, Meta Inc., and Google [4].

However, most of the available data is related to a very limited number of companies and organizations that form almost an oligopoly – the so-called Big tech companies: Alphabet, Meta, Apple, Amazon, Microsoft, and Tesla [5], [6], [7]. For Small and Medium Enterprises (SMEs), it is much harder to extract the same value from their data compared to these large enterprises due to three main challenges: (a) they have no access to such an amount of data, (b) they have not access to the technology to process the data, and (c) they have not the knowledge to transform their traditional business towards data-driven business models [8]. To cope with these challenges, we *introduce the concept of data marketplace ecosystems* in this paper.

A data marketplace ecosystem is a specific concept marketplace. Various data marketplaces already exist in different shapes and can be categorized along multiple dimensions, making a general classification of the multiple forms of business models difficult. In [9], a comprehensive model incorporating various dimensions for categorizing electronic marketplaces is proposed. For the categorization of electronic marketplaces in our work, we consider this model (see Figure 1).

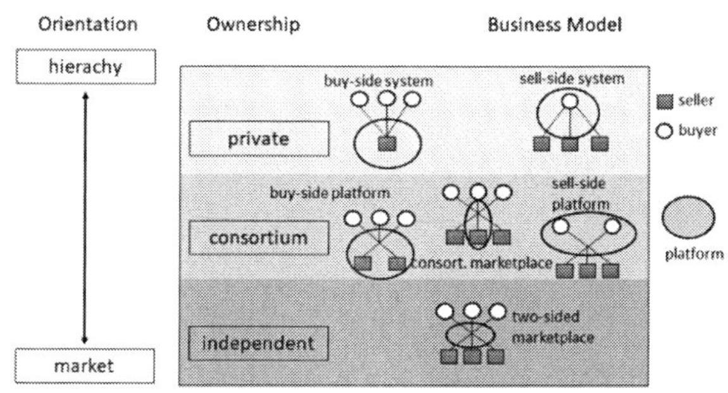

Figure 1: A taxonomy for data marketplaces from [9]

In this model, first, providers are placed on a scale of orientation between hierarchy and market, as shown in figure 1. Economies have two basic mechanisms for coordinating the flow of material or services through adjacent steps in the chain: markets and hierarchies. Markets coordinate the flow through supply and demand forces and external transactions between individuals and companies. Market forces determine the design, price, quantity, and target delivery schedule for a given product that will serve as an input into another process. On the other hand, hierarchy coordinates the flow of materials through adjacent steps by controlling and directing it at a higher level in the executive order rather than letting market transactions conform to it. Managerial decisions determine the design, price, quantity, and delivery schedules at which products from one step on the chain. Thus, all transactions between suppliers and buyers can be classified as either hierarchical or market-based.

Furthermore, data marketplaces are categorized based on their ownership (see figure1), which can be (a) private, i.e., owned by a single company (seller or buyer); (b) consortia-based, i.e., owned by a small number of companies (seller or buyer); and (c) independent, i.e., the marketplace is run as a platform without any connection to sellers or buyers.

The last dimension in the model of [9] differentiates between six business models. As shown in figure 1. at the hierarchy level are the privately-owned platforms. These types of business models typically facilitate the selling and buying of its owner, i.e., a company, and only allow one-to-many and many-to-one relations. The consortia-based platforms are between; these models typically collaborate with various companies and facilitate their buying and selling methods. Many-to-many marketplaces are usually operated by independent parties and have minimal entry restrictions at the market level.

According to [9], most of the currently existing data marketplaces, like knoema.com or mdm-portal.de, have a hierarchy private or hierarchy consortium-based business model, see figure 1. Consequently, a single company, organization, or a small consortium of companies and organizations have control over the data marketplace – that is what we define as an *ownership data marketplace*.

As a result, the buyer and the seller have to trust the owner of the marketplace, which is a major problem, as it cannot be ensured that the data will not be misused. One example of this is the Facebook-Cambridge Analytica data scandal in early 2018, where they used personal data for political advertising without the consent of the users [10].

To avoid this, in contrast to an ownership-controlled data marketplace, we *propose our concept of a Community-driven data marketplace, i.e., a data marketplace ecosystem*. A data marketplace ecosystem does not belong to a single authority and is instead owned and controlled by a *community system*, part of the marketplace. The community system itself is open such as new participants may join the different communities and thereby contribute to and supervise the data marketplace and its evolution. Therefore, the data marketplace ecosystem comes with an *open business architecture platform* that provides the technical foundation for transparency and trust by enabling peer-to-peer transactions for the whole data marketplace ecosystem. The community system has various responsibilities that help define, develop, and evolve the open business architecture platform. These responsibilities are the *relationship between the community system and the open business architecture platform*.

The rest of the paper is structured as follows: Section II gives a brief overview of the state of the art of data marketplaces, software ecosystems, and technologies for transparent and trustable peer-to-peer business transactions. Section III presents our concept for a data marketplace ecosystem that is driven by a community. Section IV summarizes and gives insights into future work.

II. STATE OF THE ART

This Section aims to present an overview of the current state of the art in data marketplaces on the one hand and software ecosystems on the other hand. Finally, blockchain technology and smart contracts are introduced since our blueprint is based on these technologies.

A. *Data marketplaces*

A data marketplace ecosystem is a specific concept for a data marketplace. Like any data marketplace, a data marketplace ecosystem is an electronic marketplace to trade data. An electronic marketplace is commonplace for interaction between *sellers* and *buyers*, where interactions determine the price and quantity of goods. Moreover, the marketplace provides infrastructure for trading. Marketplaces are concrete locations that facilitate the market. A marketplace is an infrastructure that enables the abstract concept of a market. A market serves three primary functions: First, it serves as an institution, i.e., it assigns roles such as buyers and sellers. Provides trading protocols and governs the behavior of the participants. And finally, a market defines the process of transactions [1]. Thus, an electronic marketplace, also known as e-commerce, is an infrastructure or concrete agency that allows participants to carry market transactions via an electronic medium. As in a data marketplace, transactions and other market processes such as buying and selling data are carried out through an electronic medium. In general, a *data marketplace* is a platform for trading data [11]:

- It provides an infrastructure for trading.
- It allows sellers to sell data.
- It allows buyers to buy data in exchange for money.
- It defines the trading protocols and the transaction process.

Moreover, the existing data marketplaces can be classified into two categories [12]:

1. Marketplaces are more motivated by the Internet of things devices, which allow subscribing data, such as *data.iota.org* or *streamr.com*. Here the Stakeholders deal with *Real-Time Data (RTD)*, where the buyers need real-time data or a subscription to real-time data, e.g., traffic data for a navigation application.
2. There are platforms and marketplaces like *kaggle.com, knoema.com, redliondata.com,* or *dataandsons.com,* and even more, where users can find *Non-real Time Data (NRT)* which we define as datasets. For example, this data can be used to train an Artificial intelligence model or make a forecast based on historical data.

Real-time data will increasingly turn into a commodity in the coming years. Intending to provide real-time data, Streamr is an RTD marketplace. Anyone can publish events to data streams, subscribe to streams, and use the data in decentralized apps. Much of the data is free, but the terms of use are stored in Ethereum smart contracts [13].

The IOTA Marketplace is a decentralized data marketplace that aims to make IoT data available to any compensating party. The main goal is to solve the following 3 challenges [14]:

1. Producing an initial, open-source Proof of Concept
2. Exploring new IoT/M2M solutions and business models for the "Economy of Things"

3. Growing a co-creation ecosystem to foster permissionless innovation

The Mobility Data Marketplace (MDM) enables different parties to offer mobility data, such as petrol prices or motorway construction sites [15]. Compared to Streamr, Datum and the IOTA Marketplace, MDM is not based on any cryptocurrency or blockchain technology behind and is a closed system.

In recent years, many ideas have been proposed to give back the power to the consumers to decide whether they want to share their data. One such project is Datum; the Datum Client empowers users to take control of all their data and optionally share or sell their data through the Datum network [16].

Another NRT Data Marketplace is Synapse AI, which comes up with the idea that users can sell their personal data to train AI Applications. It is built like many other solutions on blockchain technology [17], [18].

Current research focuses on NRT data marketplaces, designed decentral and usually based on blockchain technology. The main field of application is the exchange of IoT data, and the research objectives are generally ruled by reference architectures [19], [20], [21].

Most of the actual NRTD Data marketplaces are quite closed systems, where the sellers especially have to trust the organization behind it because they have to upload their datasets there. In addition, as already mentioned, this trust has been tarnished, at least since the *Facebook-Cambridge Analytica data scandal.*

The RTD marketplaces are mostly still a work in progress and used mainly for pushing some cryptocurrencies behind them, even though there is now no data marketplace known where a Buyer can find RTD and NRT in one marketplace. Another disadvantage of the work in progress RTD marketplaces is that they are designed for cryptocurrencies, and Users can only pay with these currencies. Still, most actual cryptocurrencies are volatile, which has a powerful impact on the market. Moreover, the introduced data marketplaces are private or consortium-owned. The RTD marketplaces, based on blockchain technology, are also owned by the consortium behind their cryptocurrency. The blue area shows where most of the, I.e., ownership data marketplace exists, and the red site offers our approach towards a community-driven, I.e., a data marketplace ecosystem.

B. *Software Ecosystems*

An ecosystem in nature is the relation and the balance between organisms and their environment, and the environment directly influences the life and the development of the organisms [22]. This concept can easily be transferred to software systems that consist of several independent components, so-called software ecosystems.

The interest in software ecosystems in research increased rapidly from 2010 until today, as shown in a literature Study by Konstantinos Manikos 2015, who has analyzed 231 papers about software ecosystems. The research papers mainly focus on "architecture" (which means software architecture), and another focus was variability, integration, quality, and requirement engineering [23].

One of the main reasons for a software ecosystem is the large variety of configuration options, which give the user a high degree of freedom. Some examples for software ecosystems are the Linux kernel, Debian, Eclipse and Android [24].

Even though most ecosystems have the same goal of being as open as possible, they differ greatly in the organizational structure behind them. To tackle the question of how to provide an open and independent system on the one side, but also provide a fixed and secure framework as well as rules on the other side, there different kinds of organizational structures [23], [24]:

- Monarchy: The ecosystem is orchestrated by one actor.
- Federal: The ecosystem is orchestrated by a set of representative actors.
- Collective: The ecosystem is orchestrated through processes involving all the actors, e.g. voting Anarchy: the ecosystem is characterized by the lack of a general orchestration and each actor acts on their own, based on local needs.

Other research work speaks not only of the software ecosystems but also of IT ecosystems in which machines, IoT devices and humans are considered more part of the overall system. So, IT ecosystems are complex adaptive Systems of Autonomous Systems [25]. I(o)T ecosystems extend software ecosystems' challenges with hardware interoperability and more robust semantical gaps [26].

The term Software ecosystem was first described by David G. Messerschmitt and Clemens Szyperski in the book of the same name and defines software ecosystems as a set of businesses functioning as a unit and interacting with a shared market for software and services, together with relationships among them [27]. In this, the challenge is to bring ecosystems together with business models.

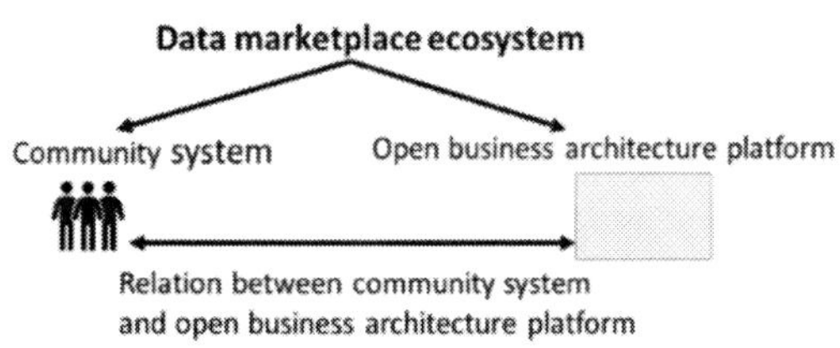

Figure 2: Overview of a data marketplace ecosystem

The actual research and the challenges in the software ecosystem are like our problem. Moreover, delegating control to a community follows the same approach as our concept. Therefore, we introduce a data marketplace ecosystem, as shown in figure 2. based on the already done and ongoing research in the field of the software ecosystem. The data marketplace ecosystem has a community system and an open business architecture platform. The responsibility of the community system with regards to the open business architecture platform is the relationship between them.

C. *Technologies for transparent and trustable peer-to-peer business transactions*

1) Blockchain: In recent years, a new technology called blockchain evolved, which has the potential to provide a trustworthy, secure platform for peer-to-peer transactions. Blockchain enables distributed, transparent way of communication. On an abstract level, a blockchain is a distributed ledger that allows users to send data and verify it without a central entity [28]. Blockchain, at its core, is a distributed and decentralized open ledger that is cryptographically managed and updated by various consensus protocols and agreements among its peers [29].
2) Smart Contracts: Researcher Nick Szabo was the mid-1990s, first conceived the concept of smart contracts. Nick Szabo describes smart contracts as a set of promises specified in a digital form, including protocols within which parties will perform what promises. Thus, the essential components of a smart contract are [30]:

- A set of rules or promises
- It is in a digital form
- The Protocols for communication and performance are defined
- Performance of actions is triggered automatically.

Blockchain provides a platform to run smart contracts. Thus, enabling automatic execution of contracts on behalf of the users. But it is important to note that smart contracts and blockchain are different ideas. A blockchain can exist without smart contracts, too e.g. bitcoin is a blockchain application that exits without smart contracts. However, smart contracts and blockchain enable many new possibilities, which were not achieved until now. Blockchain provides two out of the four important components for smart contracts i.e. a protocol for communication and performance of actions between various parties and a digital form. Further, the first concept of smart contracts related to blockchain technology is exposed on the blockchain, which is quite a problem regarding privacy. But now, there are also ways for smart private contracts, as an example, hawk a decentralized smart contract system that does not store financial transactions in the clear on the blockchain [31].

III. Data Marketplace Ecosystem

In this Section, we present our overall concept of the data marketplace ecosystem, see figure 3. The main components of the ecosystem are on the *community system,* the *open business architecture platform,* and the *relation between* them which builds together the *data marketplace ecosystem.*

A *data marketplace ecosystem* is a decentralized, open and large software system owned, controlled, and used by a community system. It consists of the following components:

1. A *community system* is a group of people who share a common interest but still form a heterogeneous system. The community system can be subdivided into different homogeneous subgroups.
2. The *open business architecture platform* is the platform i.e., the data marketplace itself, which the community systems develop, operate, and use. IT describes the technical realization of a whole system for a data marketplace ecosystem. A blueprint for this will be presented in Section 3.3, but first, we introduce the community system.
3. The responsibility of the community system for the open business architecture platform is the *relation* between the community system and the open business architecture platform.

Along with having an open architecture and community-driven, the data marketplace ecosystem is also open for integration. It provides not just the buyers and sellers a platform to exchange data but also an open architecture for developers to integrate various services according to user requirements. Because of these various services, the marketplace users are not restricted to using just one predefined service but can rather use a variety of options. E.g., to sell the data is not to be converted in a format that the platform supports. Still, the developers can offer various services for selling and storing data in many different formats and types. The same applies to payment, and the developers have the opportunity to integrate various payment options and offer them as services.

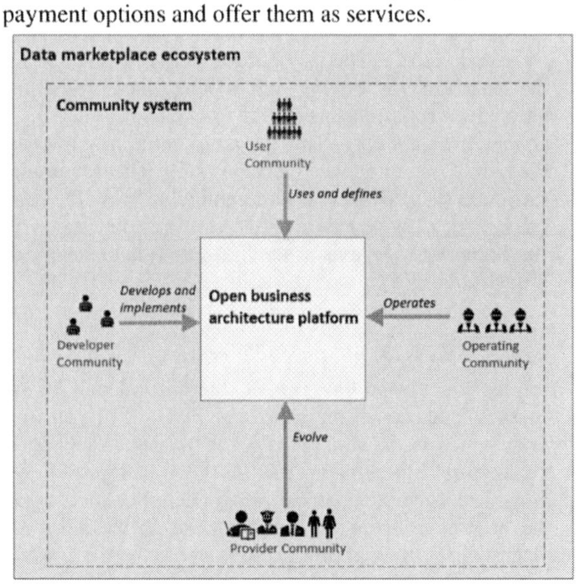

Figure 3: Overview of a data marketplace ecosystem

A. *Community system*

To avoid an *ownership data marketplace*, controlled by a single authority or small consortium, our concept of a data marketplace ecosystem is Community-driven. In order to achieve this objective, it is also necessary to ensure that the organizational structure behind the ecosystem is not monarchial. For this, we propose a *community system.*

As mentioned earlier, the community system consists of various communities performing different tasks and having various responsibilities. All these communities together build the data marketplace ecosystem. We define the community system of a data marketplace ecosystem into the following four communities:

1. *Provider community:* A not anarchical ecosystem requires some authority of control. As it is a goal of this system is to be as open as possible. We propose the provider community, which gives them control of the system to the users and benefits many other services or developers who want to integrate the services in the data marketplace. However, not everything can be combined. The services various services one hand, do not restrict the buyers and sellers, but not every service cannot be integrated because it might imbalance the ecosystem or introduce a threat to the ecosystem. Thus, the data marketplace needs some rules and standards. The provider community defines rules for the data marketplace ecosystem, e.g., a service to be offered on the marketplace should meet some standards. The provider community defines these standards and validates if the services meet them whenever it wants to be integrated into the platform.
2. *Developer community:* The developers create different services that can be integrated into the data marketplace to fulfill user requirements. Their task is to build new services that are in line with the data marketplace ecosystem.
3. *User community:* The users of the data marketplace use the platform for buying and selling data. They also define new requirements for the marketplace.
4. *Operator community:* The operator community operates the data marketplace ecosystem. The operating Community provides the computation for the data marketplace to function. This is motivated to avoid single ownerships, even if they just provide the technical infrastructure (e.g., a server).

B. Open business architecture platform

Besides the *community system*, the second part of the data marketplace ecosystem is the *open business architecture platform*, which is the core concept for technical realization. An architectural blueprint for this is shown in figure 4. The individual aspects are explained more in detail below.

The central concept of this blueprint is to provide a completely *decentralized* data marketplace ecosystem, which is open and flexible as far as possible. Still, it provides nonfunctional requirements like safety, security, privacy, and dependability. In order to avoid single ownership to give control of the marketplace to the users, the system architecture is decentralized using blockchain technology at its core. This means not even one single service runs on a central server. Everything is provided by the distributed nodes and running inside them (as shown in the background of figure 4). The operator community provides the computing power and the verification from these nodes.

These concepts ensure that the whole system is entirely *distributed* and *decentralized.* Every open system needs ways to communicate with the outside and interact with its users. For this, the communication from the *open business architecture platform* to the outside is provided via interfaces, and we propose different interfaces..

The *data interface* enables the possibility to connect external data sources to the marketplace. It is motivated by two facts. First, many companies already have their own data storage system or use one from a provider they trust, and second, it increases the degree of openness. For example, this can be a simple database hosted on any random server, a cloud provider, IPFS, etc., for NRTD, and services to exchange RTD from IoT Devices or different kinds of data sources. Furthermore, an interface to other already existing marketplaces is not excluded. In addition, services can be located here. For example, check the quality of a data set or convert it to another format.

The *money interface* is based on the same idea and aims to integrate as many payment options as possible. These could be traditional payment services, like interfaces to different bank systems and online payment systems like PayPal, Alipay, or cryptocurrencies.

Both interfaces are divided into two kinds of different ports for the services. One-half of the services can access external services, and the other half not what increases the *security* of the overall system.

The core foundation interface contains services only executed within the nodes in Smart contracts. They are strictly not allowed to communicate with external services, which increases *security* and *privacy.* The developer community inside can also develop smart contracts. The *basic smart contracts* provide at least a minimum of functions that are required for a platform to build a useable system. The *developer community can develop advanced smart contracts* and become part of the ecosystem after approval by the provider community.

The mentioned services and smart contracts are divided into two different types: *The essential services* (shown in red in figure 4)-developed by the developer community- provide the minimum of functions and build the backbone of the platform and the *advanced services* (shown purple in figure 4). The idea behind this essential service is that the marketplace always has some basic minimum services which are required for it to always at least function. The advanced services in addition-developed by the developer community must meet the ecosystem standards and must be accepted by the provider community. This ensures the flexibility and expandability of the platform. The aim of the detour via the provider community is to avoid jeopardizing the overall system's stability and security and avoid illegal activities.

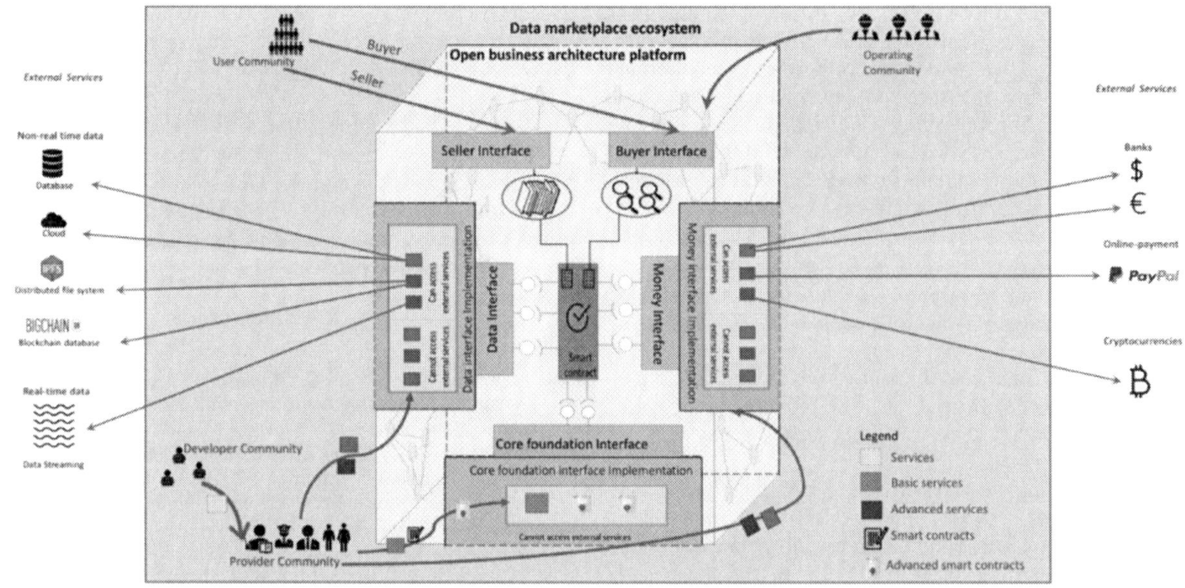

Figure 4: Blueprint for a data marketplace ecosystem

The actual users/the user community (buyers and sellers) of the marketplace access the marketplace via the *buyer* and *seller interface*, which is not a technical interface, but a user interface to get an overview of the offers, buy, or sell data. It supports the users in something of sale via the platform and configures the services according to their requirements.

C. *Relation between the community system and the open business architecture platform.*

As outlined above, the community system and the open business architecture platform build the whole data marketplace ecosystem.

This interaction and the different community system roles are essential building blocks for the platform architecture design. In fact, the developer community, for example, can implement new services, and the provider community checks them if they meet the ecosystem standards. Thus, they have different access levels to the open business architecture platform.

Figure 5 shows an overview of the relation between the community system and the open business architecture platform. As mentioned in Section 3.1 the community system has various roles and responsibilities. The user community uses the platform and creates new requirements. The developer community gets these requirements, and they develop new services based on these requirements. The services are then sent to the provider community, who can check whether these services meet the ecosystem standards. The provider community adds the services in the open business architecture platform if the services fulfill these standards. Figure 6 shows how a new service is added to the open business architecture platform and the roles the community system plays in adding them.

The *provider community* introduced as the overall control instance (comparable with the judiciary in a constitutional state) has the highest access permissions. They are also the only Community that can change the basic services, new services, and smart contracts

The *developer's Community* is comparable with the government in a constitutional state. They need permissions to build services that must interact with the interfaces and communicate with external or internal services. But to ensure the overall system's security, they do not have access to the platform core.

The *user community* (comparable with the nation in a constitutional state) cannot directly interact with the platform core and cannot implement or change services inside. They only use the application layer to interact with the open business architecture platform.

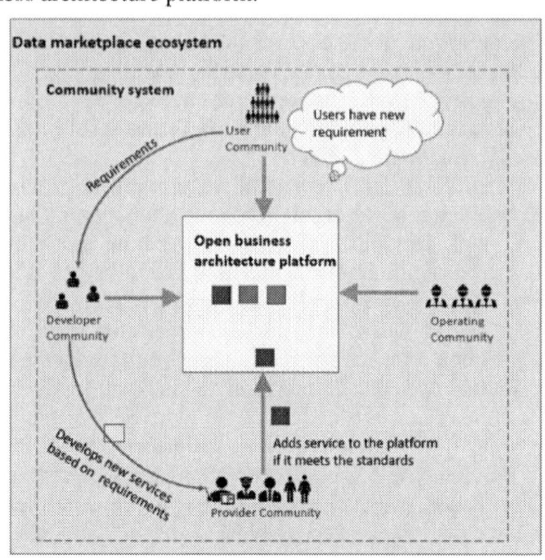

Figure 5: Overview about the relation between the community system and the open business architecture plattform

For all the introduced roles, the different community members need access permissions, which means that they must register, and a user administration service is required in the core foundation interface implementation. The only exception here is the *operating Community*. They do not have to register since they will not interact with the platform but only provide the computing power. Since it is an open system, anyone can simply participate.

IV. SUMMARY AND CONCLUSION

This non-trivial concept for an ecosystem data marketplace is based on the following basic principles in summary:

1. There is no central entity which controls the marketplace. Instead, it is governed by the community system, and the whole ecosystem is *Community-driven*.
2. The complete system is *decentralized* and *distributed*, based on underlying blockchain technology. The main reason for this is to avoid, that the services, or data inside the marketplaces are owned or hosted by a single entity. Nevertheless, other technologies can also provide these functions besides blockchain.
3. The architecture is designed to be as *open* as possible but ensures *security* and *privacy*. New services can be added via the developer community and will be controlled by the provider community.
4. The main goal of the different communities inside the community system is to avoid anarchy on the one side and monarchy on the other side. The subcommunities have the task of controlling and balancing each other.

This paper presented a blueprint for a data marketplace ecosystem based on underlying blockchain technology. The paper aimed to present a concept for a data marketplace that does not belong to a single authority.

Our concept is Community driven and proposes on the one side an initial concept for the community structure and, on the other side, an architecture that is aligned to this Community. In order to keep the marketplace as open and flexible as possible but to guarantee a solid security standard, clear interfaces are defined.

Nevertheless, this project is still a work in progress and will be continuously expanded in the near future. Our future work will include proposals about how our proposed ecosystem can be implemented and its challenges. There are already some open challenges that we identified in our earlier work. These are, for example, the final concrete organization form between the communities in the community system, the selection of the basic services, and a lot of open questions about how to increase the stability and the security of the whole system. Further, we identified in our previous work some main challenges related to data marketplaces, which we still want to provide solutions for in the data marketplace ecosystem. Some of these challenges are, e.g., how to check and guarantee data quality or automatically generate metadata for the product offer [32]. Especially for dealing with data quality, we proposed a core concept where buyers can define requirements and an intelligent contract, which holds this requirement and the dataset and verifies the compliance.

ACKNOWLEDGMENT

This research was funded by the German Federal Ministry of Education and Research (BMBF), grant number 033R240C (project title "EffizientNutzen—data-based business models for the cascade usage and extended product usage of electr(on)ic products").

REFERENCES

[1] L. Atzori, A. Iera, and G. Morabito, "The Internet of Things: A survey," *Comput. Networks*, vol. 54, no. 15, pp. 2787–2805, 2010.

[2] Jeff Desjardins, "How much data is generated each day? | World Economic Forum," 2019. [Online]. Available: https://www.weforum.org/agenda/2019/04/how-much-data-is-generated-each-day-cf4bddf29f. [Accessed: 20-Jun-2021].

[3] A. Hasty, "Treating Consumer Data Like Oil: How Re-framing Digital Interactions Might Bolster the Federal Trade Commission's New Privacy Framework," *Fed. Commun. Law J.*, no. April, pp. 293–324, 2015.

[4] Lucy Handley, "Amazon beats Apple and Google to become the world's most valuable brand," 2019. [Online]. Available: https://www.cnbc.com/2019/06/11/amazon-beats-apple-and-google-to-become-the-worlds-most-valuable-brand.html. [Accessed: 18-Jun-2021].

[5] Z. Abrahamson, "Essential Data," 2014.

[6] Jennifer Fraczek, "Facebook, a 'data monopolist'? | Business| Economy and finance news from a German perspective | DW | 15.07.2014," 2014. [Online]. Available: https://www.dw.com/en/facebook-a-data-monopolist/a-17788350. [Accessed: 18-Jun-2021].

[7] Vince Cable, "The tech titans must have their monopoly broken – and this is how we do it | Vince Cable | Opinion | The Guardian," 2018. [Online]. Available: https://www.theguardian.com/commentisfree/2018/apr/20/tech-monopoly-apple-facebook-data-extreme-content. [Accessed: 18-Jun-2021.

[8] M. Saam, S. Viete, and S. Schiel, "Digitalisierung im Mittelstand: Status Quo, aktuelle Entwicklungen und Herausforderungen," Zentrum für Europäische Wirtschaftsforschung (ZEW), Mannheim, 2016.

[9] F. Stahl, F. Schomm, G. Vossen, and L. Vomfell, "A classification framework for data marketplaces," *Vietnam J. Comput. Sci.*, vol. 3, no. 3, pp. 137–143, 2016.

[10] Carole Cadwalladr and Emma Graham-Harrison, "Revealed: 50 million Facebook profiles harvested for Cambridge Analytica in major data breach | News | The Guardian," 17-Mar-2018.

[11] M. Travizano, C. Sarraute, G. Ajzenman, and M. Minnoni, "Wibson: A Decentralized Data Marketplace," pp. 1–6, 2018.

[12] P. R. A. Lawrenz, Sebastian; Sharma, "The Significant Role of Metadata for Data Marketplaces." 2019.

[13] "Streamr vision," 2017.

[14] Cara Harbor, "Part 1: IOTA Data Marketplace—Update – IOTA." [Online]. Available: https://blog.iota.org/part-1-iota-data-marketplace-update-5f6a8ce96d05. [Accessed: 13-Jun-2019].

[15] P. Stieler, V. Kanngiesser, and F. Hilti, "MobilitätsDatenMarktplatz-welche Chancen ergeben sich für

Städte und Gemeinden?," *Agit - J. für Angew. Geoinformatik, 1-2015*, pp. 204–210, 2015.

[16] R. Haenni, "Datum Network The decentralized data marketplace," 2017.

[17] D. P. Gailey, "Synapse : Decentralized Intelligence List of Figures."

[18] "Synapse AI: AI economies on the blockchain Whitepaper v1.0," 2018.

[19] C. Perera, C. H. Liu, and S. Jayawardena, "The Emerging Internet of Things Marketplace From an Industrial Perspective: A Survey," *IEEE Trans. Emerg. Top. Comput.*, vol. 3, no. 4, pp. 585–598, 2015.

[20] L. M. De Rossi, N. Abbatemarco, and G. Salviotti, "Towards a Comprehensive Blockchain Architecture Continuum.," *Proc. 52nd Hawaii Int. Conf. Syst. Sci.*, vol. 6, pp. 4605–4614, 2019.

[21] K. R. Ozyilmaz, M. Dogan, and A. Yurdakul, "IDMoB: IoT data marketplace on blockchain," *Proc. - 2018 Crypto Val. Conf. Blockchain Technol. CVCBT 2018*, no. June, pp. 11–19, 2018.

[22] P. Monga, Radhika, and D. Sharma, "Structural and Functional Unit of Environment: Ecosystem," in *International Conference on Recent Innovations in Engineering, Science, Humanities and Management (ICRIESHM*, 2017, pp. 275–280.

[23] K. Manikas, "Revisiting software ecosystems Research: A longitudinal literature study," *J. Syst. Softw.*, vol. 117, pp. 84–103, 2016.

[24] T. Berger *et al.*, "Variability mechanisms in software ecosystems," *Inf. Softw. Technol.*, vol. 56, no. 11, pp. 1520–1535,2014.

[25] A. Rausch, J. P. Müller, D. Niebuhr, S. Herold, and U. Goltz, "IT ecosystems: A new paradigm for engineering complex adaptive software systems," *6th IEEE Int. Conf. Digit. Ecosyst.*, pp. 1–6, Jun. 2012.

[26] A. Bröring *et al.*, "Enabling IoT Ecosystems through Platform Interoperability," *IEEE Softw.*, vol. 34, no. 1, pp. 54–61, Jan. 2017.

[27] D. G. Messerschmitt and C. Szyperski, *Software Ecosystem: Understanding an Indispensable Technology and Industry*, 1st ed., vol. 1. The MIT Press, 2005.

[28] A. M. Antonopoulos, *Mastering Bitcoin: Unlocking Digital Crypto-Currencies*, 1st ed. O'Reilly Media, Inc., 2014.

[29] Z. Zheng, S. Xie, H. Dai, X. Chen, and H. Wang, "An Overview of Blockchain Technology: Architecture, Consensus, and Future Trends," *Proc. - 2017 IEEE 6th Int. Congr. Big Data, BigData Congr. 2017*, no. October, pp. 557–564, 2017.

[30] N. Szabo, "Smart contracts: building blocks for digital markets," *EXTROPY J. Transhumanist Thought,(16)*, vol. 18, 1996.

[31] A. Kosba, A. Miller, E. Shi, Z. Wen, and C. Papamanthou, "Hawk: The Blockchain Model of Cryptography and Privacy-Preserving Smart Contracts," in *Proceedings - 2016 IEEE Symposium on Security and Privacy, SP 2016*, 2016, pp. 839–858.

[32] S. Lawrenz, P. Sharma, and A. Rausch, "Blockchain Technology As an Approach for Data Marketplaces," in *Proceedings of the 2019 International Conference on Blockchain Technology*, 2019, pp. 55–59.

Qualitative Monitors based on the Connected Dependability Cage Approach

Felix Helsch*, Iqra Aslam†, Abhishek Buragohain‡, and Andreas Rausch§
Institute for Software and Systems Engineering
Clausthal University of Technology
Clausthal-Zellerfeld, Germany
Email: { felix.helsch*, iqra.aslam†, abhishek.buragohain‡, andreas.rausch§ } @tu-clausthal.de

***Abstract*—Many Autonomous Systems (ASs) have been widely applied in safety-critical applications like driverless taxis and financial credit assessment. Due to the integration of machine learning techniques for functions like environmental perception, ASs are nowadays a hybrid construction combined with classical engineered and Artificial Intelligence (AI-) based subsystems. Such a construction of the hybrid AI-based AS makes it impossible for engineers to guarantee the dependability requirements during development, since the system cannot be completely tested and formally verified. Addressing these dependability issues of the hybrid AI-based AS, this paper provides a transparent overview of our Dependability Cage approach on different levels of abstraction. In particular onboard continuous monitoring is combined with remote technical supervision for human intervention in our approach for Runtime System Observation and Resilience System Stabilization, forming a *Connected* Dependability Cage. The Qualitative Monitor for observing the system's functional correctness at runtime is chosen as an implementation example and is evaluated in the concrete use case of the research project "VanAssist" which focuses on using AVs for package delivery in urban areas.**

Keywords*—Dependable Autonomous System; Connected Dependability Cage; Runtime System Observation; Resilience System Stabilization; Qualitative Monitoring

I. INTRODUCTION

Autonomous Systems (ASs) have recently achieved success in many application domains, including automated vehicles (AVs), smart home systems, and autonomous financial agents. They are getting increasingly useful and beneficial for us. As a side effect, we as the users rely on the services of such systems increasingly, even in safety-critical applications such as driverless taxis and financial credit assessment [1] [2].

Many recent improvements in the performance of AS are made by using machine learning techniques [3]. Such a system design makes AS nowadays become hybrid Artificial Intelligence (AI-) based systems, consisting of classical engineered subsystems and machine-learned subsystems based on Artificial Intelligence (AI) techniques. Automated vehicles as an example, the AV's perception is mainly realized based on AI and the feedback control is designed as classical engineered subsystem. Both system parts are integrated on an AV to perform the expected safety-critical tasks.

A. Motivation

Considering the engineering perspective, there are various differences between the classical and the AI-based systems [4]. The classical engineering process for safety critical applications starts with a (semi-)formal requirements specification that must be complete and correct. While this idealized process is rarely realized to its full extend, the requirements specification is later used as main input for the system's testing and verification. For the development of an AI-based system, a huge data collection is used instead of the requirements specification. Different from the completeness and correctness of the requirements specification, the data collection is incomplete and may even contain a small percentage of incorrect data samples.

Nevertheless, these AI-based systems are widely applied for the fulfillment of safety-critical tasks. Product liability regulations impose high standards on manufacturers regarding the safe operation of such systems [5]. Against such a background, established engineering methods are no longer adequate to guarantee the dependability requirements (safety, security and privacy) in a cost-efficient way due to significant limitations. For instance, they are not able to handle the specific aspects of AI-based systems, as discussed in [1]. Thus, engineers cannot completely test and verify AS during development to fully guarantee the dependability requirements.

In the development of AI-based systems like the AV's perception, engineers use labeled training data and machine learning techniques to train an interpretation function. For illustration, a simplified perception task that classifies the traffic signs to the corresponding semantic classes is shown in Figure 1. For this purpose, a machine learned interpretation function needs to be trained using the training data to map a finite set of input data (e.g., traffic sign images) to the correct output information (e.g., traffic sign classes). Machine learning abstracts from the given training data examples and produces the machine learned function that is able to process an infinite number of different images. Thus, the resulting machine learned interpretation function can map any kind of image taken by the camera in a real environment to one of the known traffic sign classes. Considering the AS's operation from a safety perspective, an essential question is whether the produced output information of the machine learned interpretation function $if_{ml}(x)$, processing the current input data x, is sufficiently reliable to be safe.

Different from the AI-based systems, classical engineered systems are developed by using a (semi-)formal requirements

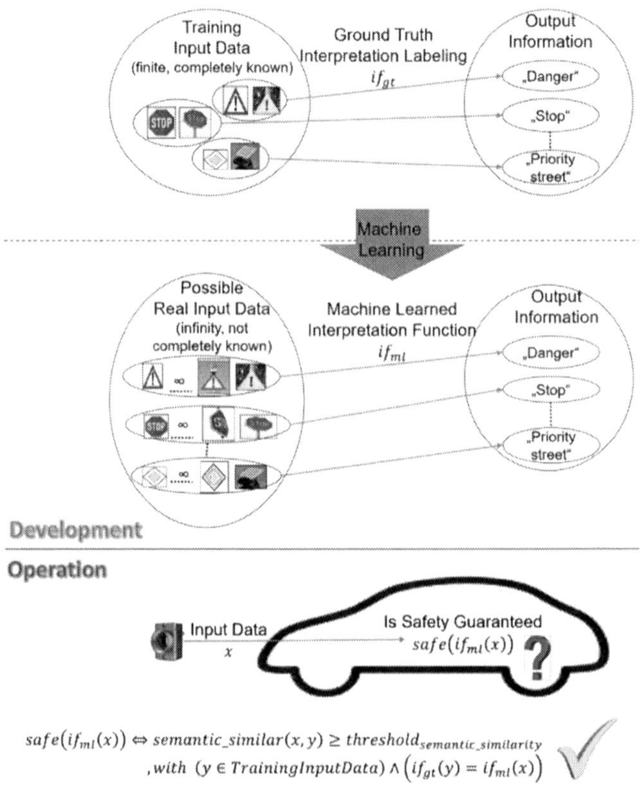

Figure 1. Check of Dependability Requirements for AI-based Systems. [6]

specification to describe the systems' behaviors, as introduced before. In this case, the behaviors must conform to the specification and thus it can be verified if the system meets the requirements. Such engineered behaviors are desirable for most types of systems like information and cyber-physical systems. However, the classical engineering approach is not applicable for AI-based ASs due to the use of a huge data collection instead of the (semi-)formal requirements specification. Even if a requirements specification is available, AI-based systems are not only expected to adhere to their specification but also solve problems more effectively by acquiring new skills with their online learning capabilities. For this purpose, ASs need to learn from the experienced situations and accordingly adapt themselves. In addition, such an adaptation and learning capability is especially essential for ASs designed for highly complex tasks, since the problem domains of the automated driving cannot be fully specified during development due to their incredible high complexities. An analog example in our real life to get a rough estimation of the high complexities is that a human driver needs many years of driving experience to be able to assess potentially dangerous traffic situations.

In contrast to traditional systems, adaptive and learning systems also entail risks and challenges. While the classical system behavior is predictable and comprehensible, the behavior of adaptive and learning systems can possibly deviate from the behavior specified during the system development. For example, the Twitter bot TayAndYou was launched by Microsoft in 2016 as an experiment to communicate with people [7]. It was supposed to learn from the conversations with Twitter users and adapt itself accordingly. But the bot only learned to curse and scold other people. Such behavior were neither planned nor expected by the system designers.

Based on the fundamental concepts of adaptive and learning systems, it has to be accepted that, we cannot completely specify and predict the behavior of such kind of systems. Due to incompleteness of the specification and uncertainty of the operational environment, as discussed above, it is not possible to test, verify or validate these systems exhaustively during development. Thus, we need to identify new ways to monitor adaptive and learning systems, and develop standard procedures to verify their behaviors' correctness. To sum up, the core challenge is: How can we guarantee safe and secure behavior for all parts of an AI-based AS (e.g., complex functions, machine learned functions, sensors and actuators, and the whole system), if the system operates in an unknown environment and do behavioral changes due to online learning have an impact on dependability requirements during operation?

B. Previous and Related Work

In order to tackle the challenges of engineering dependable hybrid AI-based ASs the Dependability Cage concept was proposed [8] [9] [10] [11] [12]. Dependability Cages are derived by engineers from existing development artifacts. The derived Dependability Cages are then used both during the ASs development and operation to check the fulfillment of dependability requirements. This approach aims to give the users a transparent view of the confidence level.

The Quantitative Monitor as an essential part in the Dependability Cage concept was proposed in [6]. As illustrated in Figure 1, the Quantitative Monitor intuitively indicates whether the AS is currently processing actual real input data x, which are from a reliability perspective similar enough ($semantic\_similar(x, y) \geq threshold_{semantic\_similarity}$) to the (ground truth) training input data (y) used for machine learning techniques, so that the produced actual output information of the machine learned interpretation function $if_{ml}(x)$ can be assumed to be correct and safe. If this is not the case, the AI-based AS is possibly in an unsafe state.

In this case, providing a measure for the semantic similarity of input data that serves as an argument for the output information reliability is a challenge. Novelty detection to automatically identify new relevant test data differing from the available training data becomes an interesting approach to realize such a semantic similarity measure. One promising novelty detection approach using AI technique called autoencoder have been proposed [13].

The basic principle of autoencoder-based novelty detection was introduced by Japkowicz et al. [14]. In their approach, the autoencoder is trained to minimize the error between an input image and a reconstructed input image. Firstly, known images were used to train the autoencoder. After training, the autoencoder was fed with new images. If the difference between original and reconstructed image was higher than a given threshold value, the new image was classified as novel [15] [16].

However, a big structural difference in input data does not necessarily correlate with a different output information class. For instance, as illustrated in Figure 2, completely different traffic situations (output information class) frequently have similar images (input data). While the AV is free to pass the zebra crossing in Figure 2a, in Figure 2b it instead has to stop and let the pedestrians pass the crossing.

(a) AV can pass (b) AV has to wait

Figure 2. Similar camera images of pedestrians represent very different traffic situations [6] [17].

In the previous sections, different challenges with respect to the engineering of hybrid AI-based ASs were identified. A high level concept for these challenges, which we also applied to our Dependability Cage was set up in [8]: The identified challenges pointed out two types of risks that have to be considered through all development phases of the AS: (1) external risks due to the uncertainties in the system's real operation environment, and (2) internal risks caused by the system's changing behavior. In the aforementioned Dependability Cage concept, two categories of Dependability Cages were defined to safeguard against these risks: (a) Dependability Cages developed for the system and (b) Dependability Cages for the system's environment. In order to use these Dependability Cages, a distinction is made between several types of behaviors of the system and its environment both at development time and at operation time.

At development time a given AS and its environment are further differentiated into its engineered behavior and its tested behavior (cf. Figure 3 left).

Similarly to the development time, at operation time a differentiation is made between the real behavior and the observed behavior of a given AS and its environment (cf. Figure 3 right). The real behavior means the behavior at operation time which may differ from the engineered behavior. It contains an uncountable number of situations caused by different influencing factors. For an AS, the real behavior is based on the system adaptation to the constantly changing operational environment. For the system's environment, the real behavior is determined by the environmental uncertainty due to unforeseeable situations that may occur during operation. The observed behavior is a subset of the real behavior and

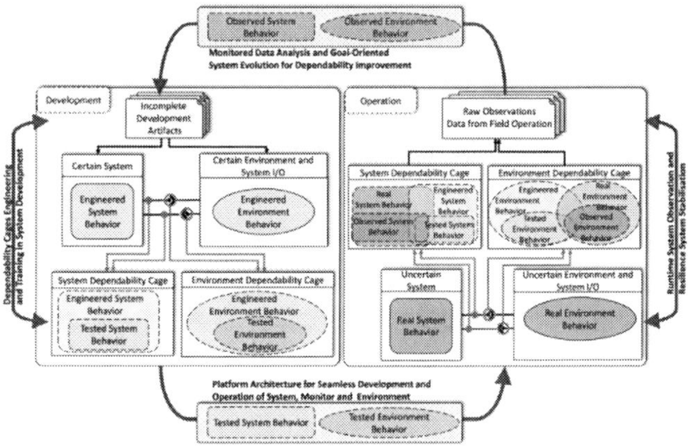

Figure 3. Dependability Cages: Overall approach. [8]

represents the behavior monitored at operation time through the Dependability Cages.

Once the tests at development time are completed, the tested behavior is transferred into operation time via a platform envisioned for this purpose (cf. Figure 3 bottom). In turn, the observed behavior is channeled back to development time to augment the development artifacts and contribute the AS's evolution, and consequently, the improvement of the system's dependability through further training of the Dependability Cages (cf. Figure 3 top). Thus, the Dependability Cage approach consists of four major parts:

- Dependability Cages Engineering and Training in System Development
- Runtime System Observation and Resilience System Stabilization
- Monitored Data Analysis and Goal-Oriented System Evolution for Dependability Improvement
- Platform Architecture for Seamless Development and Operation of System, Monitor and Environment

Due to the scope of this paper, we will discuss only the part of Runtime System Observation and Resilience System Stabilization.

C. Section Overview

This paper is organized as follows: In the following sections we will describe our connected dependability cage concept on different levels of abstraction. Section II defines the high level components of our Dependability Cage which we use for Runtime System Observation and Resilience System Stabilization and especially also introduces the remote operator for the *Connected* Dependabilty Cage concept. Following up on that, Section III introduces a more concrete architecture with lower level components for the VanAssist Project. And finally in Section IV we demonstrate our Connected Dependabilty Cage concept on the use case of the VanAssist project and concretize the realised implementation.

II. The Core: Runtime System Observation and Resilience System Stabilization

As introduced before, one of the major parts in the Dependability Cage concept is the Runtime System Observation and Resilience System Stabilization. The core element of this part is an onboard continuous monitoring framework, as shown in Figure 4. For reasons of simplicity, we depict the architecture for automated driving systems by following the input-processing-output pattern along a well-known high-level reference architecture established previously [18] [19] [20]. This reference architecture consists of three parts: (1) environment- and self-perception, (2) situation comprehension and action decision, and (3) trajectories planning and vehicle control.

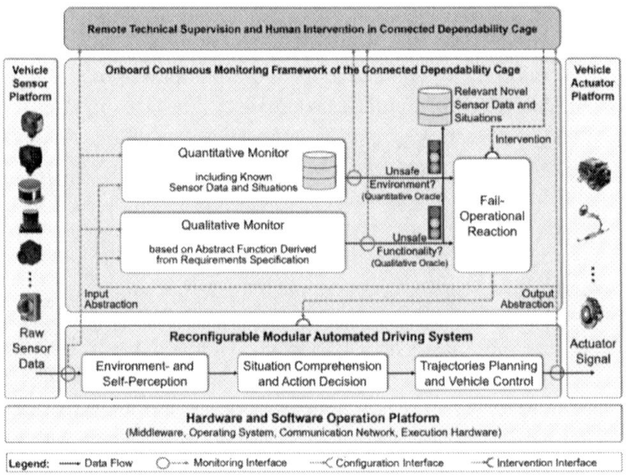

Figure 4. Runtime System Observation and Resilience System Stabilization in the Connected Dependability Cage approach based on [6].

The monitoring framework focuses on two issues: (a) does the system show correct behavior in terms of dependability requirements (Qualitative Monitor) and (b) does the system operate in a situation and environment that has been trained or tested during development (Quantitative Monitor)?

Both monitors require consistent and abstract data access to the system under consideration, with the help of the input and output abstraction components. They depict the interface between the AS and the two monitors. Both, the input and output abstraction components use defined interfaces to access the AS's data and transform it into abstract representations. Abstract representation types and values are derived from the requirements specification and dependability criteria of the AS.

The Qualitative Monitor evaluates the correctness and safety of the system's behavior under the assumption that (a) the system operates in a situation and environment that conforms to the requirements specification, and (b) the system consists of an abstract behavior function and a conformity oracle. The abstract behavior function calculates a set of correct and safe actions in real-time for the system in the current abstract situation. The conformity oracle compares the output abstraction with the set of correct and safe abstract actions from the abstract behavior function. For applications of the Qualitative Monitor, we refer to the work of Grieser et al. [21] and Mauritz et al. [9] [11].

The Quantitative Monitor observes the encountered abstract situations. For each situation, the monitor evaluates in real time if the encountered abstract situation is already known from development. A knowledge base provides information about tested situations on an abstract level. A canonical representation of abstract situations is used in this study. These canonical abstract situations are considered to be unique situations. For further details about the Quantitative Monitor, we refer to the work of Rausch et al. [6].

If one of both monitors either identifies an incorrect and unsafe system behavior or a novel situation (outliers), safety measures must be initialized to guarantee dependability requirements. For this purpose, a Fail-Operational Reaction component is designed in the monitoring framework to immediately transfer the failed system into a safe state with acceptance of appropriate risks, e.g., following the approach of a graceful degradation like in [22].

In addition to the initialized safety measure, the system data are automatically logged, which will be used as artifacts during the system's further development, aiming to analyze and eliminate previously unknown faulty system behaviors and thus increase the system's testing scope. Relying on such a process flow of runtime system observation and a continuous iterative development process, a so-called resilience system stabilization is realized.

In the reality, it is utopian that the onbaord continuous monitoring framework based on the technical system can handle all critical cases of the automated driving system. Thus, a redundant monitoring element, a so-called Remote Technical Supervision and Human Intervention is proposed in the Dependability Cage concept from the safety perspective. The Remote Technical Supervision and Human Intervention plays the role of a complementary consultant of the onboard continuous monitoring framework, so that a remote human supervisor can lively access current situations of the AVs during their operations. In the case that the current problem cannot be solved locally by the fail-operation activity of the onboard monitoring framework, a human intervention of the remote supervisor can be performed, e.g., by manually choosing an appropriate fail-operational reaction. Such a monitoring and supervision concept with redundancy massively increases the AV's safety. Moreover, the Remote Technical Supervision and Human Intervention also enables to remove the required onboard safety driver from the AVs, following the draft bill for the german traffic rule law [23]. Thus, the Remote Technical Supervision and Human Intervention work together with the onboard continuous monitoring framework and constitute an cooperative solution of a so-called *Connected* Dependability Cage concept. Since the Remote Technical Supervision and Human Intervention is not located on the AV, interfaces to a communication infrastructure are designed, so that we will now speak about a Connected Dependability Cage.

III. Instantiation of the Connected Dependability Cage for real World Applications of Automated Vehicles

The Connected Dependability Cage approach as a generalized concept addresses the safety domains of different automated mobility solutions. In reality, different domains have their constraints and boundary requirements like hardware setups, regulations, and physical performance limits. To evaluate the approach's feasibility, we applied the concept of Runtime System Observation and Resilience System Stabilization in the overall approach by instantiating a more concrete architecture. The instantiated architecture is designed considering the use case of the research project VanAssist [24].

A. Use-Case Definition

The project VanAssist aims to develop an integrated vehicle and system technology that enables largely emission-free and automated delivery of goods in urban centers. This project focuses on how automated transporters for delivery of goods can helps to optimise the daily jobs of postmen by creating optimized routes which are not possible in the classical manner. For further information about the project VanAssist, we want to refer to [24] and the VanAssist website [25]. Since misbehavior of the automated transporter can lead to hazardous situations, such a system is considered a safety critical system. In such a safety critical system, an overall safety architecture is required to guarantee that a so-called minimal risk condition is reached in case a hazardous situation happens [26]. However, in such states the monitored system tends to not be able to continue its mission and might cause traffic jams for instance. To avoid such undesired behavior in the project, the previously mentioned Remote Technical Supervision and Human Intervention is required, which is implemented as a Remote Command Control Center to acquire and supervise the AV's context information and realize the human intervention if necessary. Thus the Remote Operator shall always get enough information about the AV's context, which is mainly provided by cameras. Within the use case, we addressed the following safety requirements:

1) The AV shall never drive against or over obstacles
2) Camera data of the AV shall never be invalid

In the project, a goods delivery transporter – the Platform for Future Urban Mobility and Transport (PLUTO) – with an automated driving system was developed as an evaluation platform by the Automotive Research Centre Niedersachsen in Germany [27]. The PLUTO serves as an evaluation platform in the project VanAssist and is configured as an automated goods delivery transporter. For environmental perception four fish-eye cameras and eight high-performance LiDARs are used to create a surround view with 360° degrees.

B. Instance Architecture of Dependability Cage in the Use Case

Since the aforementioned safety requirements address the functional correctness of the automated system, the Quantitative Monitor concept (cf. Section II) with another safety goal was not applied in the project. Instead, the Qualitative Monitor and the Fail-Operational Reaction in the onboard runtime monitoring framework and the remote technical supervision were derived as the main aspects of the instantiated architecture.

The instantiation of the Connected Dependability Cage is driven by the use case defined above and thus addresses automated vehicles using LiDARs and cameras to perceive local environmental information and is based on the work of Raulf et al. [28]. The instance of the Connected Dependability Cage is depicted in Figure 5.

The instantiated system architecture consists of three subsystems: (a) A Reconfigurable Modular Automated Driving System that performs the driving task and provides reconfiguration interfaces, (b) a Dependability Cage that executes the onboard Qualitative Monitoring and the Fail-Operational Reaction at runtime, and (c) a Remote Command Control Center with HMI for the offboard supervision and human intervention by a remote Teleoperator. In addition, the Remote Command Control Center also provides interfaces to external entities to constitute a more complicated networked architecture consisting of multiple Connected Dependability Cages.

As illustrated in Figure 5, the automated driving system is the target system under runtime observation by the Connected Dependability Cage and Remote Command Control Center, which can be seen as a cooperative human-machine monitoring system for the safeguard of the automated driving system. Once the automated driving system detects a hazardous situation, the monitoring system would trigger an appropriate reaction and perform a reconfiguration via the interface provided by the driving system. Depending on concrete cases of the detected hazardous situations, the responsibilities between the Dependability Cage for onboard runtime monitoring and the Remote Command Control Center would be dynamically changed. Both can also be understood as redundant monitoring systems (respectively onboard and offboard) that aim to minimize the safety risk as far as possible.

In the following, we will focus on the internals of the instance architecture from Figure 5. Due to the scope of this work, we will only focus on the internals of (b). Within (b) the Qualitative Monitor consists of three components: "Safe Zone", "LiDAR Detector" and "Camera Validator". Whereas the Fail-Operational Reaction consists of one component: the "Mode Control".

The component "Safe Zone" is designed to determine areas, in which obstacles shall not occur based on the physical characteristics like the dynamic driving behavior and stopping distance based on the steering angle and current speed of the monitored system. Thus the *Safe Zone* remarks hazard areas in which obstacles shall not occur when performing the dynamic driving task. This component is an generalisation of the work of Grieser et al. [21] to determine a monitoring area and can consist of subzones which can correlate with driving modes.

The component "LiDAR Detector" focuses on the fulfillment of safety requirements relevant to the LiDAR-sensor. It checks if obstacles are in the *Safe Zone* or in specific subzones based on LiDAR point cloud(s). If an obstacle is identified,

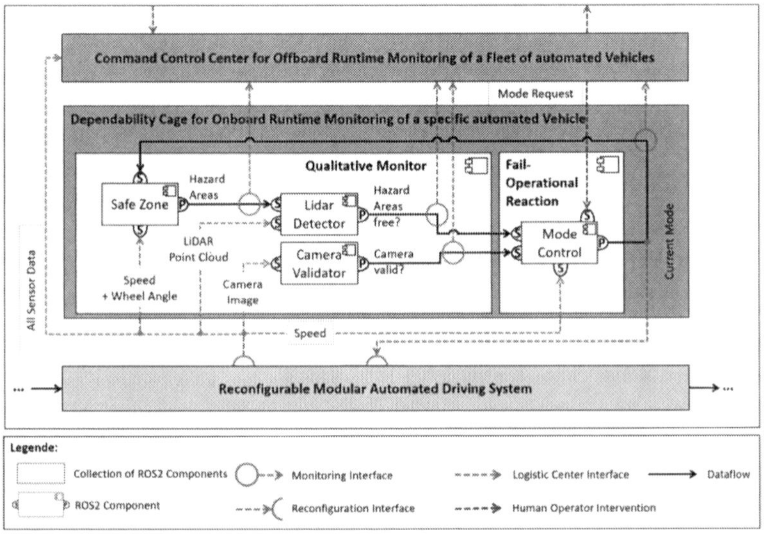

Figure 5. Instance of the Connected Dependability Cage based on [28] for automated vehicles using LiDARs and Cameras to perceive local environmental information.

a trigger is caused, which is consumed by components of the Fail-Operational Reaction. To safeguard the automated driving system and the Remote Operator from unusable camera data, the "Camera Validator" checks if camera data is valid and causes triggers for a Fail-Operational Reaction in the case of invalid data.

The "Mode Control" was derived as a component of the Fail-Operational Reaction and is responsible for determining an appropriate driving mode based on the current situation. The driving mode can be either a nominal, a degradated or a safe mode and directly correlates with instances responsible for overall system safety. The selection is based on triggers caused by the Qualitative Monitor and other necessary information correlating with driving modes.

IV. Detailed Concepts in the Instance Architecture

In the previous section, we introduced a safety architecture called Connected Dependability Cage for automated vehicles which uses LiDAR and camera sensors for the environmental perception. One main part, the Qualitative Monitor, continuously monitors the selected Automated Driving System. In this section, we will focus on the Qualitative Monitor implementation and will explain the motivation and concepts of the components within this safety architecture(see Figure 5). Additionally, we will provide a proof of concept in the scope of the two safety requirements presented in the previous section using PLUTO [27] as a demonstration platform. In the following, we will call the PLUTO AV.

To fulfill the safety requirements, the Qualitative Monitor shall (a) detect hazardous situations in the AV's surroundings and (b) detect invalid camera data produced by the AV's cameras. Once a violation is detected a fail operational reaction is triggered. Following the safety architecture of the Connected Dependability Cage in Figure 5, the implementation of the Qualitative Monitor M_{quali} can be represented in a functional description as follows:

$$M_{quali}(v, \alpha_{steering}, P_{li}, I_{cam}) = f(Z_{safe}, D_{li}, V_{cam}) \quad (1)$$

$$D_{li}(Z_{safe}, P_{li}) = f(z_{state}) \quad (2)$$

$$V_{cam}(I_{cam}) = f(c_{state}) \quad (3)$$

$$Z_{safe}(v, \alpha_{steering}) = f(Z_{clear}, Z_{focus}) \quad (4)$$

v	current AV speed
$\alpha_{steering}$	steering angle of the outer front wheel
P_{li}	LiDAR point cloud
I_{camera}	camera image
z_{state}	Zone state (free/blocked)
c_{state}	Camera state (valid/invalid)
Z_{clear}	Clear Zone (inner zone)
Z_{focus}	Focus Zone (outer zone)

Taking the safety requirements, the AV's hardware setup and physical attributes into account, we took the work of Grieser et al. [21] as a starting point and extended it, resulting in the development of a "Safe Zone" component Z_{safe}, a "LiDAR Detector" D_{li}, a "Camera Validator" V_{camera} and a "Mode Control" component.

A. Safe Zone

The purpose of the "Safe Zone" Component is to calculate a hazard zone around the AV, as shown in Figure 6 and Figure 7. In addition to the main hazard zone, we also defined an outer hazard zone, which has larger offsets to all sides. This was used to demonstrate the concept of graceful degradation like in [22]. To differentiate between these two zones, we introduced the terms *Clear Zone*, for the main hazard zone and *Focus Zone*, for the outer hazard zone. The most important information required to calculate these hazard zones are the vehicle's trajectory, its direction of driving and the stopping distance.

Since the approach for calculating the stopping distance is the same as in the previous work of Grieser et al. [21], we only briefly recapitulate this part in the first subsection. In the later subsections the generalized zone shape and the derivation of the corresponding parameters are described in more detail.

Stopping Distance

The calculation of the stopping distance of the AV is based on Ackermann steering geometry. For the basic calculation of the stopping distance, we are just listing the formulas 5 through 11 and for a more detailed description of this part of the approach, we refer to Grieser et al. [21].

Stopping distance s_{stop} (and intermediate results) for straight driving:

$$s_{stop} = s_{reaction} + s_{brake} \tag{5}$$

$$s_{reaction} = v \cdot t_{reaction} \tag{6}$$

$$s_{brake} = \frac{v^2}{2 \cdot a_{brake}} \tag{7}$$

$s_{reaction}$	distance travelled during the AV's reaction time
s_{brake}	distance travelled during the AV's braking time
$t_{reaction}$	estimated worst case reaction time of the AV
v	current speed of the AV
a_{brake}	braking deceleration of the AV

Stopping angle α_{stop} (and intermediate results) for curved driving:

$$\alpha_{stop} = s_{stop}/r_{mean} \tag{8}$$

$$r_{mean} = (r_o + r_i)/2 \tag{9}$$

$$r_o = d_{axle}/sin(\alpha_{steering}) \tag{10}$$

$$r_i = \sqrt{r_o^2 - d_{axle}^2} - d_{wheel} \tag{11}$$

r_{mean}	mean value of outer and inner radius
r_o	distance from the center of steering M to the outer front wheel
r_i	distance from the center of steering M to the inner back wheel
$\alpha_{steering}$	steering angle of the outer front wheel
d_{axle}	distance from the center of the back axle to the center of the front axle
d_{wheel}	distance from wheel center to opposing wheel center

Zone Shape

To accommodate the perception system being able to detect objects all around the AV, we needed to generalize the concept of the hazard zone described in the previous work. While one end of the zone is still placed at the end of the stopping path, the other end is now placed at the axle opposite to the driving direction (compare Figure 6 and Figure 7).

For driving straight the resulting zone shape is still a rectangle; on the other hand for driving curved the shape was generalized to a circle segment. In the following subsections the derivation of the zone shapes is described in more detail for the different cases.

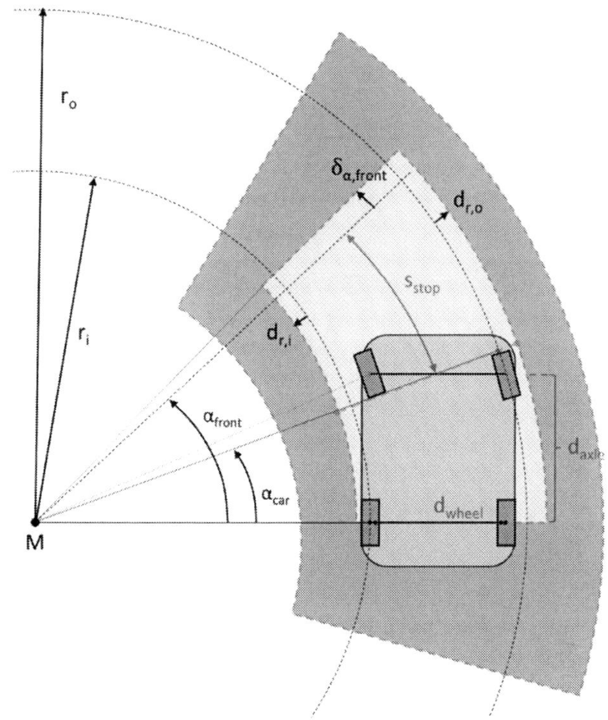

Figure 6. Forward Driving: Determination of Safe Zone with Clear Zone (green) and Focus Zone (orange).

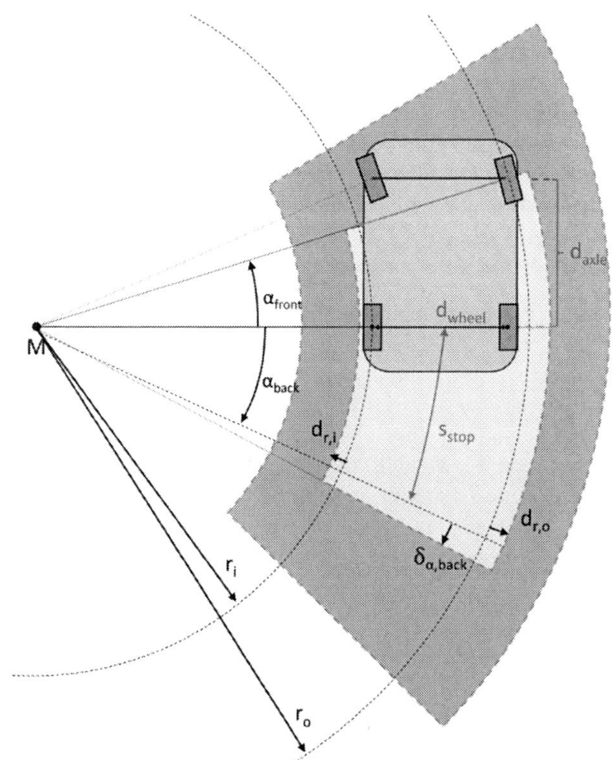

Figure 7. Backward Driving: Determination of Safe Zone with Clear Zone (green) and Focus Zone (orange).

Driving Straight

In the case of driving straight, the width of the zone is given by the wheel distance d_{wheel} plus a safety offset (on both sides). Whereas the length of the zone now is the sum of the axle distance d_{axle} and stopping distance s_{stop}, again plus a safety offset.

Driving Curved

Overall the zone for driving curved is described by four parameters: The inner radius r_i, and the outer radius r_o. The angle α_{back}, which starts the circle segment at the back side of the AV and the angle α_{front}, which ends the circle segment at the front side of the AV.

Outer radius r_o and inner radius r_i are always calculated by formulas 10 and 11, which are already used for the basic stopping distance calculation. The derivation of the other parameters is described in the corresponding subsections for the different cases.

Driving Curved, Forward

For the case of driving forward (see Figure 6) the starting point of the back angle is placed on the rear axle, so that:

$$\alpha_{back} = 0 \tag{12}$$

The starting point for the stopping distance is placed in the center of the front axle, so that the total front angle α_{front} is the sum of the stopping angle α_{stop} and the angle α_{car} to the front of the car:

$$\begin{aligned} \alpha_{front} &= \alpha_{car} + \alpha_{stop} \\ with \quad \alpha_{car} &= atan(r_i + d_{wheel}/2) \end{aligned} \tag{13}$$

Driving Curved, Backward

For driving backwards (see Figure 7) the back angle is directly equal to the stopping angle, since the start of the stopping circle segment is directly aligned with the back axle:

$$\alpha_{back} = -\alpha_{stop} \tag{14}$$

And the end point of the front angle is placed at the center of the outer front wheel, which results in the front angle being equal to the steering angle:

$$\alpha_{front} = \alpha_{steering} \tag{15}$$

Driving Curved, Safety Offsets

To obtain the final set of zone parameters, we add a safety distance in all four directions in the following manner:

$$\alpha'_{front} = \alpha_{front} + \delta_{\alpha_{front}} \tag{16}$$

$$\alpha'_{back} = \alpha_{back} + \delta_{\alpha_{back}} \tag{17}$$

$$r'_i = r_i + d_{r_i} \tag{18}$$

$$r'_o = r_o + d_{r_o} \tag{19}$$

Where for example the angle $\delta_{\alpha_{front}}$ is the safety offset for α_{front} and d_{r_i} is the safety offset for r_i(analogously for the other parameters). These safety offsets are implementation specific application parameters.

B. LiDAR Detector

The "LiDAR Detector" component determines whether there are any obstacles in the *Clear Zone* or *Focus Zone* based on the Point Cloud from the eight Ibeo solid-state 3D laser scanners. For this purpose, the method of Grieser et al. [21] to determine whether there are LiDAR points in the monitoring area is extended.

Compared to the model vehicle, we faced several additional challenges for the LiDAR of the AV. The fundamental difference, is that the AV uses a 3D LiDAR setup, whereas the model vehicle LiDAR only measures two dimensional in a horizontal plane.

Consequently the ground is included in the LiDAR data and also obstacles which are higher then the AV, but still in LiDAR range. To exclude these areas, we implemented a z-cutoff, at a certain offset from the ground and a certain offset above the vehicle. In the resulting data, only z levels which are relevant for the *Safe Zone* were included, since we only want to determine if an object is in the vertical area of the zone and not where it is. This allowed us to subsequently ignore the height in the processed data and simplify it from 3D to 2D again.

Another challenge was, that the AV's LiDAR setup provides a lot more data with higher amount of details. This also means, that the data includes more points, which belong to small particles or diffusely reflected laser beams instead of actual obstacles. In the following, we will refer to these points as "ghost points". To filter out ghost points, we implemented a clustering algorithm, which clusters neighbouring points together, if their distance is smaller then our empirically determined cluster distance. Using this clustering algorithm enabled us to successfully reduce false emergency stops due to ghost points.

The result of the clustering algorithm is used in the "LiDAR Detector" in the following way: To check the state z_{state} of the zone, we determine the largest number of LiDAR points $p_{cluster}$, which are inside the rectangle/circle segment and belong to the same cluster. If this number is below the defined threshold value $t_{cluster}$, then the zone is considered as free, otherwise as blocked:

$$z_{state} = \begin{cases} free & p_{cluster} < t_{cluster} \\ blocked & p_{cluster} >= t_{cluster} \end{cases} \tag{20}$$

This test is carried out for Clear Zone as well as Focus Zone and the result is forwarded to the Mode Control.

C. Camera Validator

The "Camera Validator" component determines the validity of the raw data from the onboard camera sensor by checking whether the camera is covered or not. An algorithm is used to check the validity of the camera data. This algorithm determines the sharpness of the incoming stream of camera images, which detects that the camera is covered when the level of sharpness value falls below an empirically determined threshold value.

D. Mode Control

The "Mode Control" is a component of the Fail-Operational Reaction. It decides the current driving mode. It could be either a nominal, degraded, or safe mode, based on the "LiDAR Detector's" output, "Camera Detector's" output and the current speed of the AV. If the Qualitative Monitor components detect any problems, the "Mode Control" changes the mode from the nominal driving mode to the fail-safe mode (emergency stop). Once a fail-safe mode happens, the remote operator has the authority to select an appropriate driving mode, e.g., a degradaded mode like limited automated driving.

The logic behind the "Mode Control" is modelled as a synchronous hierarchical automata in SCADE, enabling verification of the mode logic.

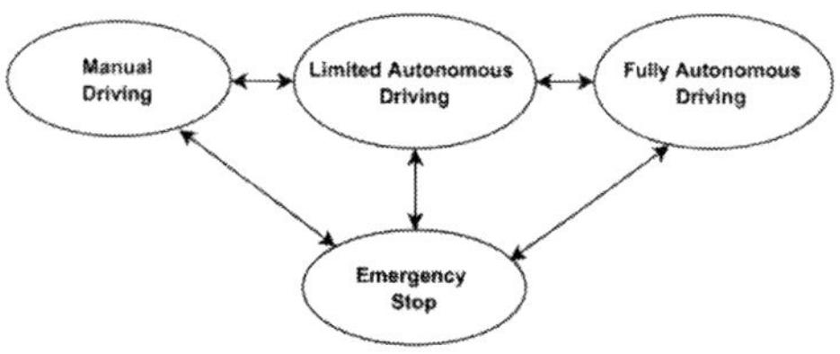

Figure 8. Simplified mode diagram of the component "Mode Control".

A simplified version of the mode diagram of the "Mode Control" can be seen in Figure 8. Due to the scope of this work, we will not dive deeper into the details of this component.

E. Implementation Middleware

Each component in the architecture, as seen in Figure 5 is implemented using the decentralized middleware ROS2 [29]. ROS2 is based on the publish-subscribe communication paradigm and provides the capability of self-adaptation and component reconfiguration. Since the AV is designed as a distributed system deployed on different ECUs, it motivated us to use ROS2. An additional point in favor of ROS2 for a safety critical system is, that it provides real-time capabilities.

F. Testing of the Qualitative Monitoring Architecture

The Qualitative Monitor is tested in two steps. First, it was conducted in a controlled environment where a track similar to the AV's test track was setup in our mobility lab using a 1:8 scaled ADAS model vehicle (similar to [21]).

As a second step, we reparameterized the *Focus Zone* and *Clear Zone* in the "Safe Zone" component for the test on the AV, since the dynamics and hardware setup vary from the model vehicle. The track considered for the test is located at the Campus Nord of TU-Braunschweig (Bienroder Weg 95, 38106 Braunschweig – for more information refer to [24] [27] and the VanAssist website [25]). Multiple test cases were derived and tested, such as driving straight, driving backward, driving at different angles, and driving towards static objects and walls. Two examples from our numerous test cases can be seen in Figure 9a and Figure 9b. In the images the LiDAR Point Cloud is visualized by black points and the *Focus Zone* (orange), and *Clear Zone* (green) can be seen around the AV, which is denoted by a blue box at the center. The indicators on the top left corner signal if the zones are free or blocked, respectively with green or red color.

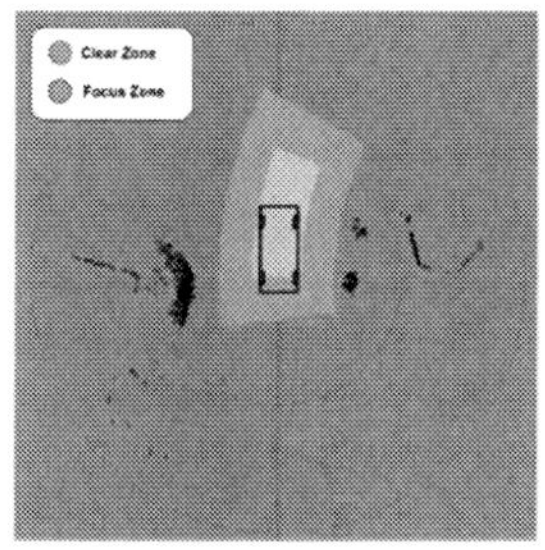

(a) Safe Zone free

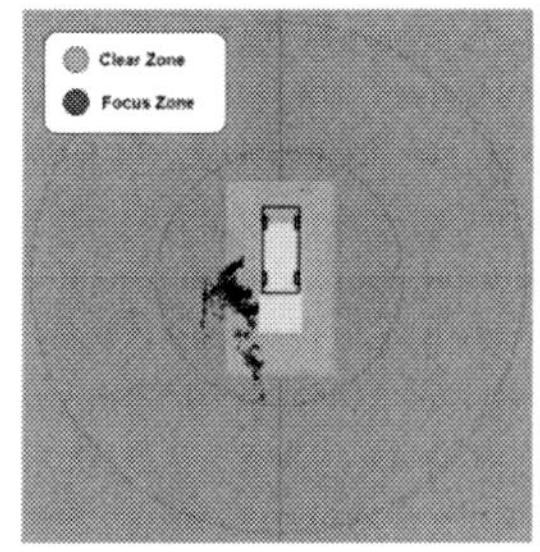

(b) Safe Zone blocked

Figure 9. Dependability Cage Test.

In the first example (see Figure 9a), we drove the AV within a curved section of the track, where no obstacles were detected by the "LiDAR Detector" within the *Focus Zone* and *Clear Zone* calculated in the "Safe Zone" component. As a result the "Mode Control" does not intervene and the AV stays in the nominal driving mode.

In the second example (see Figure 9b), The AV drove on a straight section of the test track surrounded by obstacles. These obstacles are detected as LiDAR points (black dots) inside the *Focus Zone*, but the *Clear Zone* is still free as shown in Figure 9b. Since the amount of clustered LiDAR points detected by the "LiDAR Detector" component within the *Focus Zone* is above the threshold, it resulted in the "Mode Control" triggering a fail-safe mode (emergency stop), if the nominal driving mode uses the *Focus Zone* for fail-safe checks.

V. Conclusion and Future Work

In this paper, a short overview of the Connected Dependability Cage approach is provided. As a core part, the meta-concept of Runtime System Observation and Resilience System Stabilization relying on the onboard continuous monitoring framework and the remote technical supervision allowing human supervision and intervention is introduced in detail. In addition, a concrete system architecture of the Runtime System Observation and Resilience System Stabilization is instantiated considering the derived safety requirements based on a real-world application of the AV for package delivery in urban areas. In the instantiated architecture, the Qualitative Monitor and Fail-Operational Reaction are deployed to guarantee the functional correctness of the automated driving system under runtime observation. The instantiated architecture was implemented and tested on an automated demonstration vehicle (PLUTO) in the project VanAssist. Detailed insights on the implementation were included in the paper, too.

On the way towards dependable automated driving, significant challenges that we have identified in the Connected Dependability Cage approach, are remaining. The Connected Dependability Cage allows an asymmetric assignment of AVs to the remote operators in the Command Control Center. It means that a single remote operator may supervise multiple AVs in normal operation. But the person would not be able to remotely solve the safety issues of AVs in problem cases simultaneously. Thus, an intelligent coordination and assignment between remote operators and the AV having safety issues needs to be investigated in the Connected Dependability Cage approach.

In addition, AVs under SAE Level 3+ are fail-operational [26]. For this purpose, the previously proposed concept of graceful degradation proposed by [22] for the fail-operational reaction in the instance architecture still needs to be implemented and tested. Additionally, the automated driving function shall stay within the specified Operational Design Domain (ODD) during normal operation [26], another way to further develop the Connected Dependability Cage would be the ODD monitoring.

As introduced at the beginning of this paper, ASs are nowadays AI-based. Therefore the system strongly relies on the training data without explicit requirements specifications. Thus, the Qualitative Monitor would reach its limitation to work against the safety issues due to unknown situations, which cannot be explicitly described by the requirements specifications. In this case, the Quantitative Monitor in the Connected Dependability Cage approach like presented in [6] would be a meaningful solution and needs to be implemented and evaluated in the future.

ACKNOWLEDGMENTS

This work results from the joint project "VanAssist - Interactive, intelligent system for autonomous telemonitored vans in parcel logistics" and has been funded by the Federal Ministry of Transport and Digital Infrastructure based on a resolution of the German Bundestag.

REFERENCES

[1] M. Anderson, James *et al.*, "Autonomous systems: Issues for defence policymakers," Headquarters Supreme Allied Commander, Tech. Rep., 2015.

[2] J. Youtie, A. L. Porter, P. Shapira, S. Woo, and Y. Huang, "Autonomous systems: A bibliometric and patent analysis," Exptertenkommission Forschung und Innovation, Tech. Rep., 2017.

[3] V. C. Müller, Ed., *Fundamental Issues of Artificial Intelligence*, ser. Synthese Library. Cham: Springer International Publishing, 2016.

[4] J. Rushby, *Quality measures and assurance for AI software*, 1988, vol. 18.

[5] D. Harel, A. Marron, and J. Sifakis, "Autonomics: In search of a foundation for next-generation autonomous systems," *Proceedings of the National Academy of Sciences of the United States of America*, vol. 117, no. 30, pp. 17491–17498, 2020.

[6] A. Rausch, A. M. Sedeh, and M. Zhang, "Autoencoder-based semantic novelty detection: Towards dependable ai-based systems," *Applied Sciences*, vol. 11, no. 21, p. 9881, 2021.

[7] T. Sickert. (2016, March) From hipster-girl to hitler-bot. Spiegel Netzwelt. [Online]. Available: https://www.spiegel.de/netzwelt/web/microsoft-twitter-bot-tay-vom-hipstermaedchen-zum-hitlerbot-a-1084038.html (retrieved: 2022.03.10).

[8] A. Aniculaesei, J. Grieser, A. Rausch, K. Rehfeldt, and T. Warnecke, "Towards a holistic software systems engineering approach for dependable autonomous systems," in *Proceedings of the 1st International Workshop on Software Engineering for AI in Autonomous Systems*, R. Stolle, S. Scholz, and M. Broy, Eds. New York, NY, USA: ACM, 2018, pp. 23–30.

[9] M. Mauritz, F. Howar, and A. Rausch, "Assuring the safety of advanced driver assistance systems through a combination of simulation and runtime monitoring," in *Leveraging Applications of Formal Methods, Verification and Validation: Discussion, Dissemination, Applications*, ser. Lecture Notes in Computer Science, T. Margaria and B. Steffen, Eds. Cham: Springer International Publishing, 2016, vol. 9953, pp. 672–687.

[10] M. Mauritz, A. Rausch, and I. Schaefer, "Dependable adas by combining design time testing and runtime monitoring," in *FORMS/FORMAT 2014 - 10th Symposium on Formal Methods for Automation and Safety in Railway and Automotive Systems*, 2014.

[11] M. Mauritz, "Engineering of safe autonomous vehicles through seamless integration of system development and system operation," Ph.D. dissertation, Universitätsbibliothek der TU Clausthal, 2020.

[12] M. Mauritz, F. Howar, and A. Rausch, "From simulation to operation: Using design time artifacts to ensure the safety of advanced driving assistance systems at runtime," in *MASE@MoDELS*, 2015.

[13] M. A. Pimentel, D. A. Clifton, L. Clifton, and L. Tarassenko, "A review of novelty detection," *Signal Processing*, vol. 99, pp. 215–249, 2014.

[14] N. Japkowicz, C. Myers, and M. Gluck, "A novelty detection approach to classification," in *Proceedings of the 14th International Joint Conference on Artificial Intelligence - Volume 1*, ser. IJCAI'95. San Francisco, CA, USA: Morgan Kaufmann Publishers Inc., 1995, p. 518–523.

[15] C. Richter and N. Roy, "Safe visual navigation via deep learning and novelty detection," in *Robotics: Science and Systems*, 2017.

[16] A. Alexander *et al.*, "Variational autoencoder for end-to-end control of autonomous driving with novelty detection and training de-biasing," IEEE, 2018, pp. 568–575.

[17] R. Brooks, "The big problem with self-driving cars is people," *IEEE spectrum: technology, engineering, and science News*, vol. 27, 2017.

[18] S. Behere and M. Törngren, "A functional architecture for autonomous driving," in *Proceedings of the First International Workshop on Automotive Software Architecture*, P. Kruchten, Y. Dajsuren, H. Altinger, and M. Staron, Eds. New York, NY, USA: ACM, 2015, pp. 3–10.

[19] S. Behere and M. Törngren, "A functional reference architecture for autonomous driving," *Information and Software Technology*, vol. 73, pp. 136–150, 2016.

[20] M. Maurer, J. C. Gerdes, B. Lenz, and H. Winner, *Autonomes Fahren*. Berlin, Heidelberg: Springer Berlin Heidelberg, 2015.

[21] J. Grieser, M. Zhang, T. Warnecke, and A. Rausch, "Assuring the safety of end-to-end learning-based autonomous driving through runtime monitoring," in *2020 23rd Euromicro Conference on Digital System Design (DSD)*. IEEE, 2020, pp. 476–483.

[22] A. Aniculaesei, J. Griesner, A. Rausch, K. Rehfeldt, and T. Warnecke, "Graceful degradation of decision and control responsibility for autonomous systems based on dependability cages," in *5th International Symposium on Future Active Safety Technology toward Zero*, Blacksburg, Virginia, USA, 2019.

[23] German Government. Draft law amending the road traffic act and the compulsory insurance act - autonomous driving act. Federal Ministry for Digital and Transport. [Online]. Available: https://www.bmvi.de/SharedDocs/DE/Anlage/Gesetze/Gesetze-19/gesetz-aenderung-strassenverkehrsgesetz-pflichtversicherungsgesetz-autonomes-fahren.pdf?__blob=publicationFile (retrieved: 2022.03.10).

[24] G. Seber *et al.* Final report VanAssist. [Online]. Available: https://www.vanassist.de/ergebnisse/ (retrieved: 2022.03.10).

[25] VanAssist website. [Online]. Available: https://www.vanassist.de (retrieved: 2022.03.10).

[26] S. International, "SAE J3016 - surface vehicle recommended practice - taxonomy and definitions for terms related to driving automation systems for on-road motor vehicles," 2018.

[27] T. Hegerhorst *et al.*, "VanAssist - integrated safety concept for automated vans in parcel logistics," in *ACIMobility Summit*, Braunschweig, Germany, september 2021.

[28] C. Raulf *et al.*, "Dynamically configurable vehicle concepts for passenger transport," in *13. Wissenschaftsforum Mobilität "Transforming Mobility – What Next"*, Duisburg, Germany, 2021.

[29] ROS2 website. [Online]. Available: https://docs.ros.org/en/foxy/index.html (retrieved: 2022.03.10).

International Academy, Research,
and Industry Association (IARIA)
412 Derby Way
Wilmington, DE 19810

ISBN 978-1-7138-6920-7
9 781713 869207

CURRAN ASSOCIATES INC.
proceedings
.com

Fourth International Conference on Advances in Sensors, Actuators, Metering and Sensing (ALLSENSORS 2019)

Held at DigitalWorld 2019

Athens, Greece
24 – 28 February 2019

IARIA